Mortal Divide

the
autobiography
of
Yiorgos Alexandroglou
Γιώργος Αλεξανδρόγλου

CW00460591

Mortal Divide

the
autobiography
of
Yiorgos Alexandroglou
Γιώργος Αλεξανδρόγλου

George Alexander

Photomontages by Peter Lyssiotis

BRANDL & SCHLESINGER

Text © George Alexander, 1997
Photomontages © Peter Lyssiotis, 1997
Cover image © Peter Lyssiotis, 1997

First published by
Brandl & Schlesinger Pty Ltd
24 Wilberforce Ave Rose Bay NSW 2029 Australia

National Library of Australia
Cataloguing-in-Publication entry:

Alexander, George, 1949-.
Mortal divide : the autobiography of Yiorgos Alexandroglou
ISBN 1 876040 02 5
1. Alexander, George, 1949-. Fiction. I. Title
A823.3

**This project has been assisted by the Commonwealth Government
through the Australia Council, its art funding and advisory body.**

Printed and bound in Australia by Southwood Press

For Lisa, Lola & Kiki

Acknowledgments

Thanks to Peter Lyssiotis not only for his images, that appear to have been coaxed from the ether as much as from my words, but also for his sound literary advice throughout different stages of the manuscript; to Roderic Campbell for his exemplary editorial work, both generous and astringent; to Janice Beavan for her kind suggestions and scrupulous proofing; and last, but not least, to my publishers, Veronica Sumegi and András Berkes for their patience, support and belief in this project in particular, and in independent publishing in general.

'Invenire'–to come upon–is also to invent. There are many books I have come upon that have acted as a baffle through which I was able to invent my own mortal divisions and multiplications. This novel is in some ways a cover version of a work published by Faber in my birthyear and month: Christopher Morley's *The Man Who Made Friends With Himself*, itself a somewhat avuncular cover version of many other doppelgänger stories, including those of Henry James. It is also pays tribute to Howard Nemerov's self-reflexive *Journal of the Fictive Life* (Book 2, 22. VI, University of Chicago, 1965, 1981) and a would-be homage to the underappreciated Aidan Higgins, especially his *Balcony of Europe* (Calder & Boyars 1972).

Source of other quotations

36 p. 'though they go mad...' from Dylan Thomas, "And Death Shall Have No Dominion".

64 p. 'To have contemplated...', from Marcus Aurelius, *Meditations.*

65 p. 'We go on loving...', from Violette Le Duc, *La Batarde.*

82 p. 'The desires of the heart are as crooked as corkscrews', from W.H. Auden.

86 p. 'The truth lies in several dreams...' from Pier-Paolo Pasolini, *Arabian Tales.*

97 p. 'Whatever you wanted / What can it be' from Bob Dylan, "What Was It You Wanted", *Oh Mercy.*

100 p. For the definition of *à l'anglais*, see Simon Loftus, *A Pike in the Basement: Tales of a Hungry Traveller* (London, 1987).

109 p. 'They fuck you up...', poem by Philip Larkin.

1

In this seaside suburb the houses stand empty, even though people live in them. The sand pushes south in summer with the littoral drift, and then pulls north with the winter storms and the Fremantle Doctor. The Doctor's a searing demented wind that speaks in tongues. In the teeth of encroaching dunes an unyielding will clips lawns to emerald velvet. The town itself has the papery air of a place cut out and pasted on the West Australian coast–laundromat, Safeways, videoshop, chemist. And then more sunbaked plains of sand and scrub brush.

They fear the streets here more than they do at Boot Hill or in Harlem. Gunshots heard are from daytime TV. Outside the sun rubs out reality. In Perth shadows are reality. For the boy watching TV alone the corridors of the house and the casements of the window become elusive zones. A doorbell ringing pulls the night out by its roots. Its ringing conjures masked men seen in close-up with felt-soled shoes, silent and sudden intrusions through the curtains, baseball bats brought down hard on heads, or the electric cords of domestic appliances pulled suddenly on throats.

Now there is a body just over the fence, where the fretted baize of the lawn becomes the sand dunes, a body with a great gash on the back of its head, and a few feet away one ox-blood tasselled loafer. It's as though the tormented expectancy built up over the years in City Beach had materialised a male body on the wrong side of forty that now lay half-buried in sand among the prickle lily and wild rosemary. It is as though the endlessly replayed fantasy had disgorged the police, now combing the heathlands, sectioned off by orange barrier tape, the ambulance crew surrounded by surgical trash, gauze pads, extrication collars, ventilation tubes still caked with blood.

And I? Here? Paranoia now cranked up a gear. And die here? What was I doing in this place? Meaning otherwise: what was he (robber-strangler-torturer) doing in our suburb? No time to be an outsider. This afternoon, while I sat in the borrowed Humber, the groceries on the passenger seat, a cop leaned onto the car, elbow in the window. He took details. Said he needed to pay me a visit later. Sergeant O'Hooligan: the strong underarm of the law. I have this anti-talent for being at the wrong place at the wrong time. At least my wife thinks so. Though it was her idea I should come here.

So I'm house-sitting and cat-minding. My in-laws, the Buckmasters, are travelling the white towns of Andalucia. This is where I've come to get away from a Sydney life of multiplicity, to one of simplicity. How do you explain to a cop you're in retirement from love? 'Fuck you', Alys shouted in the street wearing nothing but her bikini briefs and my leather jacket. *Fuck you I love you.*

For years the world purred with us, but now my restless behaviour was leaving marks of irritation, like a rash, on the atmosphere. I didn't want to lose her.

Everything was taking its toll. At work it was *pause-rewind-play-translate.* A bug-eyed zombie job. In the sub-titling department of a television station translating 'Good Morning Athens!' or 'Uncle Fouad's fables' or Italian versions of 'The Young and the Restless'. The scripts had to be logged in military time. Eager to coax efficiency out of us they put the unit into cells—straight lanes of fresh cubicle housing but rounded ever so gently at the corners. The same amoeboid rectangle as the video monitors and the computer keys. And the corporate promise behind each softened square or clipped circle was that it would order Babel and digitalise diversity.

Fat chance. For one thing the mind was a labyrinth. Sometimes it was one of those very dull labyrinths where the rat runs around one way and gets an electric shock and the other way he gets a grain of corn; and other days it was a labyrinth that consisted of a straight line. You could get lost in that one too. Always there were perilous seas around little islands of language, and my raft was taking in water. While translating from an Italian documentary the words *Cuore caotico delle cose, al centro del quadrato dei tarocchi e del mondo...*, which should have come out as 'chaotic heart of things, at the centre of the square of the tarots and of the world...', became a list of near-anagrams that dispersed through the script: *Cairo-Cottesloe-Kastellorizo-Karrakatta*. I cursed, switched off, wound the tape back, switched on again. At the chaotic heart of things, at the knotty centre of all representations, where memory is a labyrinth, were the key places that marked out my father's life. Kastellorizo, little Greek island off the coast of Turkey; Cairo, where he married Mum; Cottesloe, where he lived; Karrakatta, where he is buried.

11

I talked to Alys about this, and about the perilous random seas, and the waterlogged anagrams, and whether I'd make it to the Mediterranean islands or not.

Alys said: 'Go on a vacation. Vacate. Be vacant.'

She didn't know if it was the job, the insomnia or a deeper malaise that was driving us both nuts. When she met me fifteen years ago I was in grace. Took all my tasks lightly, borne along on the tide. Now I couldn't tie my shoelaces. I tried to impersonate an ordinary life: the husband who goes to the same job for ten years. But other things happen. There was this time when I'd start up making Anzac biscuits for our daughter Toto and her friends and end up with Greek funeral cakes. Where the pomegranate seeds came from I had no idea.

Worse, I came to dread bedtime. We relied on TV to not talk. TV keeps us from thinking, reminds us we have nothing to say to each other. It was no consolation that the rest of the people on the planet were living their lives in sit-coms and doing their singing in the ads. With Alys lying next to me I'd feel this overpowering desire to sleep but I couldn't. 'Let's not spoil it', she said, and took the initiative, booking me on a plane to Perth.

The doctor—Doctor Nemerov—said it would do me good, too. He said the rollers on the beach would drown out the jangled rhythms of the city and the withdrawing waves erase the clutter of timetables and schedules. And here I was watching TV coverage of TV coverage, my night-time land-scape the humming test-pattern to cover the silence and to keep me awake so I could sleep all day.

I was feeling as though I hadn't slept for months. I visited Doctor Nemerov every fortnight. He took blood and measured metabolism. He said I passed in and out of heavy sleep at minute intervals. I had what they called 'videolepsy', plunging directly into dreams whenever I closed my eyes, dreaming a bit of the story. 'You're sleeping', he said, 'but unconventionally.' He reassured me that this was quite common these days. ' "Incremental reality slippage". The technoculture's own little syndrome, when the senses no longer hold the empirical court of appeal.'

So I'm falling, but not to sleep. To some other body.

I started to worry when I woke up on a trolley in casualty at St Vincent's. They did X-rays of my skull and it was shown to be intact though I had to have stitches in my head. The day-to-day logistics of my professional life were having to be redrawn. I started to think about handing in my hard-won magnetic card to the sub-titling unit. When my co-worker Tan, the gay Vietnamese receptionist, came into the photocopy room and found me hiding in my locker, he asked me what I was doing.

'Do you saw what I see?'

'What?'

'Don't you see him?', I shouted.

'Who?'

'Yiorgos!'

'Neh, you're losing your grip', said Tan, laughing long and loud into his cupped hand.

'What do the dead want? What do they say?'

'Hai, what they always say', he said holding his hand up and shaking it loosely, 'Put yourself in my place'.

Doctor Nemerov is a Chicago MD with a golf-pro hair fix and an asymmetrical Zorro moustache. His computer terminal has a screen saver of repeating ghosts.

He gets me to close my eyes (touching me softly on the forehead) and slope under. I tell him I'm not jung or easily freudened.

'Ha ha, Germ's Choice', he says. 'Yes yes, no no', he says. 'You will speak to me directly from your unconscious. It saves time. You will hear what you say but you will not believe it.'

I'm telling him that *I can't sleep.* Everything I do becomes a form of sleep, from the rise and fall of the cigarette lifted to my lips to the dating of the policy on my household insurance... while I'm telling him all this, parts of my body start to fall asleep before others: elbows, temples, back. Everything except my voice is asleep while it tells him that a mother pushing a pram is sleep, that a politician polling a vote is a form of sleep; that a procession of Catholics eating a wafer seems like a form of sleep to me.

He asks me to describe in detail what I see as though he were a police artist. I tell him that I'm playing touch football with Blocker Roach and Fatty Vautin. We're playing with Toto's plastic toy ball, and in the stands, about the size of a postage stamp, are Dolly Parton and the film crew of *9 to 5*.

He tells me to chase information about my father's father, Yiorgos Alexandroglou. I only knew him from photographs. (Smile like a broken down broom.) I was named Yiorgos Alexandroglou myself; it is my baptismal name. My father—Kyriakos—changed it to George Alexander by deed

14

poll. When I sign my name on cheques, or place it under the title of a translated filmscript, it feels less like a signature than a faded scar.

'What's in a name?' asked Doctor Nemerov rhetorically. 'What's it mean to stuff your psyche like a sausage into Vlad or Kenneth or Kim? Nothing? Everything?'

Alys says forget about it. The Name of the Bloody Father. Why undermine this Anglo power that could protect me? In Australia, she believes, no name is foreign.

Alys says 'Yor-goss' for Yiorgos. And 'Og-glue' for Alexandroglou.

'Yiorgos Alexandroglou' (the gutteral gs brought up like phlegm from my throat) may sound like someone with thick hair on the soles of their feet to you, but to me it's like… like my total body. And that name is the distance I must travel to make friends with myself.

The last time we went to the stand-up comedy night at the Improv, Alys put that name in the bucket without telling me. Suddenly I hear 'Yiorgos Alexandroglou' and people are applauding, and I go up. I have no material. This is like a bad dream. I say the first thing that comes up: 'I'm into humiliation. The best thing you can do is not laugh!'

They crack up, and I go on about my life. That I'm a Freudian slip on legs, that really I'm an outrageously punny person. That I was born in Perth on the day of my birth, and was married they say on my wife's wedding day, and will die when I quit this earth… This old limerick bombs.

So I take advantage of the two mikes set up by the previous act. Hoping not to lose the crowd. Crowds are always between infatuations. Jumping from left to right. I do a schizo number: 'Will you join me?'. Jumping back from right to left. 'Why? Are we coming apart?' Boom boom. This rabbit punch good cheer rouses the crowd again.

'Isn't it funny how one's real life is often the life you don't lead? Have you noticed how on mike you always sound like a person trying to sound like a person talking? I can't even leave a message on my phone answering machine without feeling it's stealing my soul: 'Hi, you've just reached Yiorgos Alexandroglou's answering machine. Yiorgos has just stepped out of character for the moment, but if you'd like to leave a message...'

That was last Saturday. So here I am in Perth with a Tuesday night closing in, the sheets and pillowcases flickeringly illuminated by the pale blue glow of the television. In the house of my in-laws, by the sea. I wanted to shed clothes and complications. But far from being the clean and polished seashell of a place I'd hoped for I've ended up with more to get along with, not less. I'm in a cluttered Victorian house with a huge rolltop desk as big as a Bentley, old timepieces, oval portraits, decanters of port. The Buckmasters, Alys' parents, are probably getting pissed on the local sherry somewhere in the south of Spain.

On TV documentary footage from earthquake-ravaged Guanajouata, Mexico, showed where the dead, buried in the muddy mountain slope, had fallen out of the side, and into the local village. Then an ad (soaring music signalling the pure televisual rush of belonging to something larger than yourself). Then local news. The body at City Beach, the homicide detective trying to establish last events, last people, and who was present at the last supper before the end for this nameless man. The camera pans, bystanders stare at the spot. Remarkable in their very unremarkableness. Like any other in the heath, they stare riveted. Just that a body was left behind, like a suit. And the space it occupied continues to exist without it.

The community is shocked. Who was the Man In the Empty Shirt? A community with an established Anglophile world of Ag. colleges and cathedral weddings and holiday cottages at Rockingham. A community, a target market, a Nation to which my wife belonged with its house parties and relatives eating spotted dogs ('rolls with currants in them', explained Alys), dancing square dances ('lancers and quadrilles') and reading Parisian journals on embroidery.

I switch the TV off and pour Mr Bones, the squirming puss, from the Regency stripe couch. Reflections of a white sky and blue clouds move on the glass table. On it a photo album. I turn the pages in that ceremonial way. 'Robin skippering *Betsy* to Rottnest.' Alys' brother. What is this likeness that holds among members of a family? There's no one feature they all share, just an odd indefinite number of things that tell us she looks like the rest.

The pictures of Alys as a child in whimsical candy stripes catch my breath. Ecstatic with life unawares. Waving or beckoning or kissing her fingertips for the camera. Later more morose, intellectual, in one picture; and then somehow in the same month, sports-loving and gorgeous. One's pictorial history is deceptive. Cameras lie: that was well known. Even as they trapped a splendid spot of light on the fence forever. After that click of the shutter, gone in seconds. That smudge of duration. All that remains. Time doesn't pass, we do.

Alys' mother, Jane, came from detribalised gentry (surnames in Debrett's book of peerage). She had Iroquois cheekbones but eyes of Oxford blue. Like some women of her class she had learned to use the English language to maim. I wondered whether they were people who believed the mind was a maze or who had in perfect confidence ever taken a step down the fork where you freeze to death? Or where the road leads nowhere? It didn't seem so, yet anti-depressants set her mouth in a downward line. Mostly it was her well-meaning hubby she clobbered. Patrick was a rags-to-riches battler. His face a relief map of the Kimberleys. His family made their money hauling timber to the sawmills. Jarrah and karri out of Manjimup for sleepers, scantlings, poles, floorings, everything. Until the conservationists put an end to clear felling. The Australian story. A story that for years had defined itself against 'gyppos' and 'gins'.

The words 'bung' and 'gin' are written underneath a photo in which Aborigines are running alongside a train that passes through reserves. There are scattered mia-mias and bush breaks made from ringed water tanks, and iron wheel rims. And white man's barbed wire cutting into powerful Rainbow Serpent country. Country where the mundane stones are the food eaten and where objects have an attracting force, and certain people, like the kadaitcha men, are the earthly batteries for that energy. But that was before the colony was, well, civilised.

In the bathroom Mr Bones is licking the salty armpit of my denim shirt. From the window I see a shining beach rim through the grove of Norfolk pines. Behind, two houses away in the backyards, kids fling themselves at each other, or try and skim on their boogie boards. Our swimming pool is quiet except for the 'Kreepy-Krawly' hissing and vibrating along the bottom and sides. Like some beautifully evolved sea-creature it slurps its way along the tiles, sending concentric ripples around the dead insects floating on top: bees, marchflies,

spiders. In moments when the AC cycle shuts off a stillness blossoms. A stillness that evokes the time before suburban swimming pools and sidewalks, before viceroys and newspapers, before lawyers and margaritas. The time of the *kadaitcha* men.

Lying on Alys' old mattress in the guest room I was tormented by solitary harems. Wife, *weib*, weaver of desire. My lover, I love her and yet she says I'm sick. I need the space and the time 'to get earthed'. Earthed? Plugged into the damp sand of corruption beneath us, the blood-soaked earth?

'Every grave is a gramophone.'

'A classic syndrome of paranoid psychosis.'

'Psychosis?'

'The "p" is silent. As in bathing.'

She kept appearing that night in disordered dreams in ludicrous disguises; as Zoë, or Isabella Rossellini in *Wild at Heart*, or as her daddums in a platinum wig and clipped moustache. The dreams were like messages on paper gone at the folds, the characters inhabiting a country where prankish children had turned all the signs around.

3

At City Beach a small crowd had gathered. Stepping over the police barrier tape, men with walkie-talkies and holstered revolvers beneath suit jackets hustled a hatless man in a khaki greatcoat and granny glasses inside the scrum of council officials, ambulance men and cops. They called him Dr Death. He was Inspector Belacqua Toth. Homicide. He was new to Western Australia but had a reputation. He was an expert in all dark matters. Older detectives more streetwise, younger ones more erudite, stepped aside in certain cases for the otherwise apparently dull Belacqua Toth.

Within days of his arrival in Perth they gave him a junkie's tour of the inner city. As a joke they teamed him up with Bluey, an ex-skinpopper, whose mix of front and terror made him a jumpy sidekick. Together they trawled the backstreets talking to the young muggers and petty hoods, the addicts and affectless lechers. Bluey rang the doorbells and gave the passwords, crashed the shooting galleries and the sly grog shops while Belacqua's street-radar flushed the racketeers and the pushers, the gamblers and the yeah-fuck-with-me hustlers on the lam.

Mystique built around a man with the name Toth. He'd worked without a badge in Tangiers. And had spent some time in the Lower East Side in New York. He had allure, pizzazz, *cojones*. But he knew how to be a blur, a cipher, a peripheral figure that melts into the surroundings.

Toth had a knowledge of men: and of women. Toth knew motives. Emotional blackmail, betrayal, fury, desolation, horror and hate. With women of all stripes he knew what buttons to press. He'd been around the block a few times and picked up quickly the shifting rules of the stone-scissors-paper game of race, sex and class. The older members of the force entered the 1990s in the way they had entered the 1950s—with a brain-dead version of manhood, slightly re-modelled into a bushwhacked jauntiness. The younger ones, vis-à-vis the sex war, no longer aspired to coherence. It was cool just to look good in tailored Italian suits. And they were mainstreaming cool with the rest of them. What they all feared, both among themselves in the corrupt force and in the social circus of Perth, was the loner. Hence all the scams, the networking, the 'psychotherapies'. Belacqua Toth was a loner. So it was lucky for George Alexander, marooned on City Beach, that it was Toth who was sent to investigate the suspicious stranger, and not some local redneck.

Had he buried some tormentor in a sandpile? This was the question for Toth. Toth could smell water or old bones buried under sand heavier than any PhD.

And so at the appointed hour, George Alexander heard a knock: loud, firm, short. He went to answer it wearily, with an odd burden (bad conscience?), or circumspectly, like a person with something sensational upon his person—say, a Ruger.

The visitor carried a grubby khaki overcoat over his arm. He still had no hat, and a face rationed as regards expression. He walked straight in, casting glances at the furnishings, and Alexander's belongings spread haphazardly all over the place.

He explained that he was here on the say-so of Sergeant O'Hooligan. He wanted to know what Alexander was doing in Perth. From then on George Alexander provided the text, Toth the glossary.

Alexander thought the detective would work all the angles, but his urbane manner made him feel and look more reliable, not less. No matter how fast you talk however, there's always something left over in your mind.

Toth was taken by the number of books in the house. He was clearly a book man. So he wanted to talk philosophy, not the hard facts. The events that fed Toth's detective imagination provided epiphanies, not clues. Clues were for the amateurs. Events were intelligent, not fortuitous. They broke like sunlight through the thickets of the mind.

He explained, 'Let's say that the man found in the sandhills with the hole in his head was dumped there by some hoods who blew a job they were in the middle of. The man had eaten a salty Turkish pizza, got thirsty, gone to a pub to buy a beer, and was murdered by hoods who happened to be in the middle of a heist. Is any metaphysical account of this event possible? The man's death was due to the chance intersection of three series of causes: one, the local history of the hoods, which brought them to the pub—perhaps they met at a police line up; two, the state of the man's digestion, which brought him to the pub; the historical facts which caused the pub—The Rose, Shamrock and Thistle—to be built on that corner. Three rigid chains of causality', and here Toth fanned out three fingers on his left hand. 'But their intersection with the man's death is uncaused in the strictest sense. It's not intelligible', he emphasised, 'but it can be accounted for'.

'Sounds scientific, and that seems to make it meaningless too.'

'And what tips life into nonsense is that it should always make sense.'

And George suddenly felt how arbitrary and contingent his muddled little nest of Alys, Toto, Sydney, money, in-laws, and friends, comes to seem! How hard these days we work at being happy; because happiness might explain everything. 'How do we make it meaningful then? These are questions that interest a writer. And, I take it, some detectives. If you were writing a book, how do you make a narrative of it? What makes it intelligible? If a tree kills your child. It's an accident and a tragedy. You kiss your wife goodbye, she gets hit by a truck. You thought she was safe. Blackout.'

'You are asking me the hard questions. What makes an event a tragedy then? And then how can a plot enclose such an impossibly complex and circumstantial conjunction of reasons? Aristotle in the *Metaphysics* answers "Pity"'.

Belacqua and George both glanced at their watches at the same time. 9:45 p.m. A chance intersection? Toth sounded as though he were quoting off the top of his head.

'Pity is the feeling which arrests the mind in the presence of whatsoever is grave and constant in human sufferings and unites it with the human sufferer. Pity? Terror? Joy? These are states of mind. A falling tree kills one's child. You blame your shortcomings as a parent; you blame some power punishing one's spiritual pride. But did a tree kill our friend on the heath?'

While he was talking the phone rang and I jumped like a man stung by a redback.

When I came back he was gone.

Perhaps he had made his mind up that I was innocent, or maybe just a lost cause. Perhaps it was only the intersecting routes through Perth that explained his errand: simultaneously accidental and determined. If everything dovetailed in one's life, like all the colours on a Rubik's cube, did that make it an epiphany? Or was it just a part of life's irony? A stone in a shoe. Every character in a book we generally assume acts in view of an end. Motives should be explicit, purposes should comply. But are we cornered by destiny? Can we exclude chance? Was the murdered man intrinsically fated to die? Was it fated to happen in such a horrible way on the heath? Is history a pinwheel, of karmic laws realised and exhausted, and of no more significance than 'a shout in the street'?

I went to the door and saw Toth's silhouette passing through the crossword diagram of the gate's shadows into the ambiguity of twilight. The xerox orange sky in the west had been taken over by a magnesia moonlight. Bones the cat, though white in colour, looked blueish in this light. While the garden looked oddly art directed, like carefully windswept hair.

For Belacqua, as he joined the ribbon of lights along City Beach Drive in his rusted Citroën *deux chevaux*, the death on the heath was not yet explicable: no light, no form, sprang from its being. The contours of a familiar story were still hard to make out in the gathering darkness, a darkness that was levelling and unifying all phenomena: levelling the miscellaneous graves of Karrakatta, and the mountain of King's Park, levelling the city by the Swan, and all the respectable men and women tucked in their beds with their memories and other fallacies.

4

The venetian blinds made tiger stripes on a naked woman lying on a couch in a sprawl. The face was a profile against darkness, a pang faintly edged with a smile, the torso poured voluptuously into convex shadows, the broad hips and legs highlighted by a slope of light.

A looking-glass tilted up from the floor reflected a camera on a tripod, black rolls of plastic sheeting, duct tape, lights, and the canvas panel of the screen on which the naked woman was depicted.

The gaze slides over the screen to a woman on the chaise, the represented woman's live double. She, in an apricot robe, rises to pull the halliard of the blind. Everything about her, in contrast to the fixed pose on the screen, is movable, moved. Zoë Ashford, artist and model, with a slightly thickened body dwells unapologetically in middle age, in the way of a Simone Signoret, or perhaps Jeanne Moreau.

Zoë removes the black wig, to reveal buzz-cut blonde white hair, and then, from her neck, the Nikon, activated by a self-timer. She goes over to the light table and peruses the transparencies—all images of erotic violence or erotic abandon. Some are staples from art history—a Balthus or Boucher, a Gauguin or Degas. Other poses are from sources more obscure and scandalous—stamped out by the cookie-cutters of the male libido.

Her work was currently occupying the small arts fraternity—and sorority. Feminist sisters weren't sure: was this masochism? exhibitionism? was this repeating or exorcising the female hostaged to patriarchal art history? Few were not moved by these bodies mobilised for collaboration.

For Zoë, acting out her sex's objectification, the fuss made was baffling. She was acting on imperatives that were both automatic and mysterious. She was, as others pointed out, both the subject and object of the gaze. She was controlling the scenarios. She was taking back the night. For her antagonists, she was flouting her lived-in body and giving guys hard-ons.

Now all that preoccupied Zoë was to finish the six hinged and movable panels of a screen for the coming Biennale of Sydney. The screen would continue to both hide and reveal the intentions of an artist as self-contained as a tigress in a fur-lined cage; as paradoxical as a shotgun covered with feathers.

Zoë went to the kitchen and prepared a salad lunch. Her building was reflected in the industrial bay of Glebe Point. The building of water seemed firmly rooted, and yet trembled in the old bay as black and mercurial as a mechanic's drip pan. Zoë loved the look of the old boathouses and the partially re-painted boats all drips and mottlings, and the half-finished hulls; loved the colour of slipways and their dripping ledges of greeny grey; the rusty sheets of iron; the derricks and bridgehouses reflected in the bottom of a sardine tin, petrol green.

Across to the west she could see a park with palms and giant Moreton Bay figs and through the glare only one moving thing: a chrome flash. As it approached the light signalled a motorbike. Moment by moment she could see the rider was Alys. The Ducati spat some gravel inside the gate. Alys called

for the keys. Zoë threw them down, Alys smiling through the
visor of the helmet.

At the top of the stairs Alys could hear the rattle of ice.
'Gin and tonic?'

Alys brought tiger lilies, and the ampoules of royal jelly
Zoë requested. They kissed.

'You taste of marzipan', laughed Zoë.
'Your breath is Cointreau.'
'Here's a letter for you.'
'From Toto!'

> dearest
> To ^ Zoë,
> Hope to see you soon when Dad trots off to
> Perth. It would be fun if you came & visited
> us (a lot!!)
> All my love, Toto.

The fiction between Alys and George is that he's gone to Perth
so he can grow up, and maybe make sense of his life and learn
to write again.

There were other reasons sure: his recovery from several
deaths, most recently that of his father, the years he's wasted at
the sub-titling unit lost between languages. His daughter
showed no interest in going to Perth with him.

But all that Alys was certain of was that she would spend
more time with Zoë. Zoë Ashford, George's *ex-* in the red
wedding dress, Alys' one-time rival, Zoë; Zoë of the several
passports and the disconcertingly direct gaze.

What made her certain were those split seconds on the dance floor at The Time Machine; there with bodies and beats flexing, the place became a parallel universe where the stages of a fatal affair could be recreated in the space of several songs. But Alys never had an inkling this rival Zoë would be in the fantastic role of lover.

'Do you think I'm cruising you?' she had asked walking home in the early hours of the morning, a time when only the council trucks were about washing the streets.

'No.'

'Good, I'm pleased we've got that straight ... so to speak.'

And now, as the sun warmed Alys face in the studio, Zoë asked, 'Is George off?'

'He's so off you can hear the flies buzzing.'

'Oh, Alys, I recall a pretty hot customer on occasions.'

'Once maybe. I'm afraid his Mr Happy has become Mr Gloom. He says the helicopter lights at The Time Machine are like too many bad Vietnam movies. He doesn't care about anybody but himself.'

Zoë touched Alys' arm and said nothing.

5

The doctor suggests that I try and tell the Yiorgos story in letters to my daughter Toto. The Writing Cure, he calls it. That might help pacify my past and pick up the plot. The writing cure for the common code.

As usual I'm in several minds about this. Not several, a few. On second thought you might say I didn't know what to think of the matter.

1929? 1950? 1989? facts, dates, happenings. An assemblage of objectivities. What can I remember? Childhood? Families? Birthdays? Names? Don't we deceive ourselves by turning lives into stories?

'With writing I am always beginning with premature disqualifications.'

'Premature … what?'

'I'm always re-beginning.'

One hundred and fifty years ago my grandfather Yiorgos got tired of packing donkey shit around the roots of other peoples' olive trees, tired of eating lentils and flapping his arms and pissing into the wind. So he left his island, off the coast of Turkey, nicknamed "In the Beginning", and packed his family off to Port Said to work on the dredging boats of the Suez Canal. Then Kyriakos, his eldest son, my father, turned his back on a desk job, spun a globe (legend has it), his finger landing on Australia, and hauled arse to Perth, sto Perthi.'

What is memory? Don't we shape events into anecdotes, incidents into adventures? Otherwise we have only one life.

The road that we travel in time is covered with the debris of all that we started to be, of all that which we could have been.

Writers, supposedly, with alternative realities available to them can push their better selves into parallel existence in print.

'I am trying to get somewhere but the words keep pointing in different directions as I go.'

'Each of us lives but one life', the Doctor says. 'We choose it deliberately, along the way, and those excluded selves we abandon come back sometimes to haunt us with their repudiated possibilities. But we can't parlay our bets on different prongs', he says. 'Write it out. Tell it as you would to a twelve-year-old', he says.

I write: 'Dear Toto'. Then write nothing. Another page: 'Dear Toto'. More nothing. 'Dear Toto' is starting to look to my eyes like 'Things To Do'.

For Toto the past was on permanent playback. *Total Recall.* Television was her fantasy of the afterlife. *Robocop.* The rest, she was beginning to learn, was non-biodegradable plastic waste dumped as landfill.

The last time Toto and I talked she was bent over her computer screen. Still in her school track-suit, she was saying: 'I want colour! I want size! This is so dinky'.

She had been adding forests and land bridges to her EcoGame. She had more grip on real-time data than I had on the days of the week. She was turning up the greenhouse effect now, and setting off volcanoes. Oh coool!

I told her not to crisp her corneas. And she said she wouldn't if I'd let her buy more megs of RAM and got a bigger screen.

This was it, enough Random Access Memory and you could move the world. Or at least contain it. Every so-called civilization—Celtic, Chinese, Levantine—soon available on a couple of CD-ROM disks at Safeways. Lots of information, but what about 'blood memory'?

All the effort over the years to keep track of names and dates of your culture—Phoenicia, Petra, Baalbek, Gaza, Jerusalem, Alexandria, Damascus, Aleppo—at the cutting edge of the Fertile Crescent. The Levant—which denotes the rising of the sun—is where Toto's forbears hailed from. A *taramasalata* of racial genes. That wonderful cross-cultural mix of Ottoman and Venetian architectures overlaid with the traces of Macedonian Greek and Caliphate Arab.

'Sure Dad', said Toto, 'I'll get someone from my generation talk to someone from your generation'.

'All the effort, Toto,' I went on, 'to pass on the telling events—when Saladin the Kurd met the Crusaders. How were those memories preserved? By memory rote first, the recitation of epic histories, passed on among caravan drivers in the deserts of Libya; and then alphabets carved into stelae, or cuneiform tablets; plus all the maps on papyrus and architectural blueprints in books ... Files of information. Information today purchasable on a few highly reflective drink-coasters called CDs.'

Would Toto be interested in this? Hardly. She makes a Yuck-fooey face. 'Can't handle your transaction right now, Dad.'

34

Toto, Totts—whose childish nape would smell of ... what? ... pancakes soaked in milk we decided. Now she smells of strawberry bubblegum and lipgloss.

Well, the past probably does all end up as a whole pile of recycled infojunk, middens for the technomads to scratch around in. According to EcoGame, from which Toto was picking up geeky *Science Times* stuff on albedo variance and lost trichlorides, the next stop after the earth smothers in its own garbage was space migration anyhow.

Civilisation was fear of entropy. Entropy the bogey man; entropy the Cookie Monster who eats birthdays; entropy with its ferocious chemical reactions.

And the message: Stay cool was the message. Refrigerate, conserve. Preferably at 0 degrees C. Stay cool and stay decipherable.

'Robocop' says Toto, 'experiences life after death through the lens of the camera. So TV is afterlife.'

Bio-tech rehearsals for leaving the body; maybe that was what we were all into. The tools of global integration—the satellite media Net, the multinational corporations—were creating an alternative, all-purpose, digital, 100% synthetic memory bank of celebrities: people in Reebok ads, veejays and deejays, game-show hosts who tell you how to lose 10 kilos, the troubled sons and daughters of show biz personalities. All familiar strangers through the fake intimacy of the boob-tube.

But, for Toto and her friends, just the kind of fertile waste to blossom into bigger, brighter, better TV.

But what about all the stories read at bedtime—oral history like Dick Whittington and his Cat (banishment); Rapunzel (sexual combat)—quite often many, many times in the exact order of words and sequences they had been read before? These were the shaping narratives, the canonical stories that we would always live by, and always want to hear again, no matter the passing parade. Once upon a time, they lived happily ever after. And in between:

> ... though they go mad they shall be sane,
> though they sink through the sea
>   they shall rise again,
> though lovers be lost, love shall not ...

Dearest Toto, Darling Tots,

I began to write to you in the morning but after breakfast the kitchen looked so untidy that I swept the floors, cleaned the sink, by which time the rest of the kitchen looked shabbier. Toto, I did the rest of the kitchen! The oven took time. By which time it had gotten late in the morning and I had to start errands. The mail arrived— then I thought of overdue correspondence. Then decided to leave writing for tomorrow. Always been a morning person (Ha!)

Next day.
Darling Toto,

Today you change cultures like TV channels. But your grandfather, my father, was part of a bridge generation of the Egyptian Exodus. I was conceived there, came of age here. I knew love in five languages. As a travelling kid you learn to be funny to trick people into liking you. Now I'm north of forty and I have my stories.

In the library of Western Australia I discovered there was a George Alexander who arrived from Liverpool on the *Otago*, June 4, 1886, with his wife Jane. Reading on I discover a William Shaw, writing back to England (March 14, 1830): 'Mr Leake a merchant in Fremantle received 300 pairs of shoes by the "Egyptian" and sold every pair in one day'—who was this Egyptian?

But things started happening. First I became deadlocked with my research on Greek migrants from Egypt. Why? Because the Department of Immigration in Perth is located in a building owned by the Kuwaiti government. Soldiers are guarding its entrance now the Gulf War is on full tilt. Three straight days of the 'Evening News'. The Middle East is miniaturised into a claymation diorama. Every target hit gets a red starburst—disturbingly painless to the eye. No connection between bombing and death.

Then there was a bomb scare in the library here—can you believe it? We were all sequestered to a corner by the windows overlooking the Art Gallery of Western Australia. Looking into the faces of my fellow Australians, none of whom have seen cathedrals burn. We're in utterly separate frames of consciousness. Our fears are coming from different sources. Our histories dispose us to different imaginings.

'What gives?'
It was him.
'What a coinky-dink.'
'Yes, what a coincidence. Chance or destiny…'
'Or both.'
'Bringing us together.'
The guy's been popping up everywhere. As though some author in Sydney had deliberately flung us in opposite directions only to end up together in Perth.

At first I had been drawn to the man's sharp profile, his swept back curls and ducktail. And then his way of appearing and disappearing with a sidelong, wary look. Outside my workplace at Rushcutters Bay: there he was getting into the taxi as I was emerging from it. At the Kastellorizian club. It's usually when I'm worrying some problem. Again I wasn't sure anymore whether I was dreaming or inventing a phantom. But I have no invention. I've been stalled on a novel for years.

'How's the book going?'
Did I say that? Or did he?
'*The Ghost Who Overstayed His Visit.* Catchy title.'
That took me unexpectedly.

'What's a ghostwriter?' he asked, all laughlines.

'Someone who writes when the spirit moves them.'

We both headed for the stairs.

'Coming or going?' he asked, offering both of us an option.

'Going', I said.

'I think we'd better spend an evening together', he said in a heavy voice.

Doctor, I promised to report. Re: Writing Cure. I must say it feels I've been too long at the keyboard already. I see my entire life as a redactable MS, both narrator and improvable character within it. My past is a 'bad book' which has to be improved; an imperfect past becomes a past historic.

Yiorgos Alexandroglou—he, me—is someone I've known for too long and ignored longer still. It's as if he's starting to get some comeuppance in these pages I'm struggling with. Already my body feels like it is doing his mind's dirty work. He's coming back. Doctor, he's coming back to reinstate his partial power. Neither alien nor friend, he thinks by writing I have given him the space for independence he hasn't had up till now.

After a Turkish pizza I had a few drinks at The Clock. A public house in Cottesloe with a simulated airport lounge, and an array of timepieces ticking off the wrong times in New York, Rome, Berlin, Hong Kong and Auckland. There was not much happening. A couple of old biddies.

'I lost Cyril. He was always walking.'

'I've got bad legs. My ankles let me down.'

On TV the Gulf War continues. The president's speech-writers strain for the calculated absence of eloquence which translates as sincerity. The very essence of WASP demeanor—silent and resolute. I'm pleased to see the blow-dried serenity of the anchormen a little frazzled though. There followed one of those insinuating financial services ads targeting people in their sixties. An old couple hiking through a rainforest. The voiceover, part Leonard Teale, part Walt Disney... *'Somehow, at some deep level, we're responsible for what happens... I mean you're the best investment you've got... Be Your Own Granite.'*

I headed home. Outside a drunk holding onto the pavement as though he were on the Manly ferry. I walk purposely in the teeth of the Fremantle Doctor past the surfclub and across the heath.

At home the clock strikes 5, then 4, then 3. The candle-flames that looked like they were guttering began to lengthen. The ceiling of my borrowed bedroom cracks into map shapes, Alexandrian maps of the East Mediterranean. Bones looks up, cameling his back around my legs, and seems to be speaking some Arabic dialect.

How could I decide any of the big questions with this going on. This sabbatical from the Multicultural Broadcasting Company wasn't helping right now. I thought of Alys; I thought of our daughter, Toto; I thought of our friends—weren't they enough? I relied on them to keep taut the thin thread of my identity.

I decide to call Alys in Sydney. Alys is the bulwark against the chaos of my life at the moment. That I know. She has a more instinctive sense of livable peace than I. For me it is always so near yet so hard to reach. Alys realises peace isn't beyond reach but inside reach. Maybe that is a birthright too, like being Australian in Australia. Alys, I felt, had been extending me more or less unconditional love. Even as the tide of feeling was ebbing of late, after the demonic waves of erotic energy couples generate in honeymoon spurts. I kept thinking of our student days and how simple life was then. It wasn't.

Now portions of our lives were being sidelined down dead ends of sense.

I speak on the speakerphone to Alys in Sydney. I tell Alys how I'm blocked with the Writing Cure, or at least spooked by it, and she says through the little mike in the machine:

'I've always been jealous.'

'Jealous?'

'Of people in books. Zoë always has such fun with them.'

'Zoë? I disagree. In artbooks maybe. People in novels often push the author around. It's a commonly observed situation.'

'You're just a little ball of Silly Putty are you, George?' There was a nasty reverb on the word *silly*.

'Sometimes I feel like I'm being written.'

'By whom?'

While on the phone I'm drawing plans of the Suez Canal. These conversations are going nowhere. In my imagination the canal leads nowhere too, used only by the engineers who built it. The canal leads to bedrock, not the sea.

In the newspaper, tabloid headlines become names that make up my life. The letters refract into different configurations. Waterlogged palindromes:

A MAN A PLAN A CANAL — PANAMA.

Men, plans, canals all going nowhere. Yiorgos went to Panama after the Suez business, and in this sleep that cannot put an end to itself I see in front of me, like old lantern slides, Indian girls naked from the waist up bathing in a rocky stream, figures brooding in cemeteries, the echo of Yiorgos among the ruins of Spanish churches...

Through the shortwave radio a jazz pianist in Tokyo deconstructs the piano back into its constituent parts: trees and rocks and elephants. I walk to the kitchen, open the fridge door and pour what I begin to think are the contents of the Red Sea down my throat.

In the mirror the world crisscrosses itself a thousand times in my face: Greek, Turk, Arab, Jew, light-eyed European.

First I hear clicking. It's Yiorgos clicking *gomboloi*, the Greek worry-beads. Then I see him. Behind me. A mirrored image gripping the doorposts with the other hand, breathing in hard loud gasps, bloodvessels corded like ropes. In waistcoat and britches. He holds the back of his head and he winks at me. An eidolon, a ghost flickering on and off. It leaves the stink of saltcod.

Toto, Wednesday.

The clock radio woke me up with more bad news in the Middle East. Itching to send you material. But Mum says we're awfully behind in bills back home and I thought I had better post some cheques. Don't want power cut off while you're in the middle of *DOOM* or whatever you're playing. Went to the bank.

Thursday. Up late. Vaguely remember talking to the Doctor. Music in the pub too loud for serious discussion in the payphone. Took long walk to clear the head. Saw many carefree people. Look over notes for book. Shot through with muddled ideas. Transitions rough. Like no clutch in car. Needs a fresh eye. Leave it alone for the rest of the day. What happened then? Forget.

I remember that night. It was the day Miles Davis died. They were playing some of his music. The DJ took out the *Get Up With It* album and played 'He Loved Him Madly', a thirty minute dirge based on an organ drone in which nothing seemed to happen. It made me both scared and calm. It had the rhythm of long journeys to hypothetical Greek islands. The music did what I wanted. It filled every corner of my being with the fine red sand of the Nullarbor. It put my mind on erase.

I started at last to write the story of Yiorgos Alexandroglou: I was born on the tenth of November in the year 1950 in the city of Perth in the state of Western Australia of Greek and Italian parents, under the astrological sign of Scorpio, the eighth house of death and regeneration. Make of it what you will, you, Toto, and my father, Kyriakos, are both Scorpios too.

Conceived in Port Said I was carried in my mother's womb like contraband sunshine through the Suez Canal, past date trees to the Port of Aden and beyond. My mother lied about how pregnant she was to get on the ship.

It was the maiden voyage for the *Orcades*, a passenger ship of the Orient Line, with its corn-coloured hull and Welsh-hat steampipe. Among the VIPs on board, was Mr Robert Menzies, then leader of the federal Opposition. He had just made a six-month tour of Europe and the USA, where he had seen the Iron Curtain, and the Soviet belligerence over Berlin and the blockade. Also on board was Peter Dawson, the Australian tenor, sitting under a sun-canopy.

At the Equator, latitude O degrees, the staff celebrated the ancient rites of Father Neptune—conjuring Dionysius and the Lord of Misrule—called 'crossing the line'. My mother in fancy dress (Marie Antoinette?) walked past the bronze panels in the saloon depicting the world's great navigators while I, a finless fish, was clamped in a dream of flight.

Does any of this help, or matter, for that matter. That I imagine these festivities at the imaginary line encircling the pregnant earth at equal distance from the poles? That I sense like faint carbon men on deck wearing huge pants and shoes like boats, while women in blooming print-dresses point to the horizon with gestures suggesting other dimensions? While ragged-tail flags wear themselves thin scraping against the sky.

These images—dreams projected on cigarette smoke—may have been provoked by a photo taken at Colombo dated 25/7/50 of Kyriakos Alexandroglou and his young wife Violetta Lo Verso. This was the first port of call East of Suez, the only speck of land to be sighted before Colombo being the coral atoll of Minicoy, rich with palm groves.

Inside the breakwater boys dived for coins thrown by the passengers. Father in an open shirt and pin-striped suit, hair tousled by the breeze, holding a coconut and a hand of sugar bananas. This was probably after an excursion to Mount Lavinia or Kandy. Mother smiling and head leaning to the left wears a floral cotton dress and cuban-heeled toe-peepers. Her right arm rests on my father's arm while in her left she carries a large straw bag. And on the tropic pavement—continuing the fertility theme— are two pineapples beside a wide-brimmed straw hat. Another photo taken the same day is dated 25/8/50. No escape from this maze of selfhood. It doesn't matter whether it was July or August, but in that margin ... I get lost. Or at least double exposed, in the gap between the facts; in that space, other appearances can be animated. When are we really born? When do we leave death? When we cry? When our parents choose a name for us?

At Dondra Head the ship would set course for Australia. Heavy rainstorms sweeping the ocean. Later the *Orcades* berths at Fremantle and the sun, a milky diffuse disc, is split in two by the water under the riveted hull of the ship. The water turns white, then green.

A prehistory of the body? Nothing is clear until Princess Margaret's Hospital, Perth, where I scream the blue bloody murder of being born.

My father arrives through the circling lens of the door of the hospital going around in glittering quadrants. A life: rushes in a minicam film.

46

Flash forward to a Perth hospital. Thirty years later, my father will leave through the very same doors: they do an embrocation to expose a vein. My father's mouth open in a naive expression of surprise, eyes fixed on something within himself.

Yiorgos—it's his voice, but I can't see the lips moving—*I'm trying to hold everything, trying to get a fix on this moment before we swing off again on the great loop-de-loops of living.*

Alone I watch as the fluid empties into a stoppered tube. Intensive Care has the cool weatherless glow of recessed lighting and the dying quail-trill of the telephones. The odour of antiseptic and fear. I go outside for a cigarette.

The gram on the cardiac monitor sloped like a téléphérique, then sagged a deep catenary, dropping out of sight. Then it reappeared, stabilising briefly like an Arabic script, the upper loops plotting the contractions of the heart, the pulse ebbing and fluttering back. *For me? Is it for me this time?*

There was a slow, strong intake of breath, and then stillness. *Eternity = Time minus Me. The rest of my life spent in the second person singular. Living the story of my life, no longer as me, but as an example of myself. I am thinking of you. The last thing I do before I sleep.* Then one more breath and he was gone.

The dead travel fast. Even as my father holds onto life with that last muscle, the heart. During that last breath like a sigh a child might give, he's dragged along by the current of time, like a tape on fast forward, or rewind. What a hullabaloo of history—what shrieks, blood, kettledrums: homes flattened, statues toppled and empty ornaments curling in intense heat, melted telephones, the charred stumps of date palms, ledger pages flapping in the wind, newspapers swirling into a heap. There's Paul the tentmaker of Tarsus spreading Christendom, and before that Pax Romana, and before that the Palace of Knossos, and before that animal muzzles rowing impassively beneath a sea of peat.

How long is biography? Nothing is very clear. It's like we're on the periphery of something vast—history—unfolding. God glides by inside a white Mercedes limo shooting video from the rear window. He pans the wreckage, gives us a V-sign, hits the window button and is swallowed up by a pane of smoked glass.

Wait. Where am I? I wake up in Bondi, 1979. The light breeze flaps the yellow curtain, tossing light then shadow. The phone call rings its bell backwards. It was mother Violetta's voice, low: 'Your father's in a coma. He collapsed on the Horseshoe Bridge.'

Some people believe we go on living in another body after our deaths. That we lived before, and some remember and some forget these past lives. I thought life was separate from death. I thought the past cut off from the present. And I expected, eventually, especially with the birth of Toto, that I'd overcome my losses. As long as there was new life I'd be immune from the depredations of death. But the dead roll on, dragging us with them, occupying our losses, incarnating the vacancies in us. We fill their absence with our substance. We become them. The dead take us over, like the hermit crab the shell of a whelk.

Es la vida. Or rather, it's death.

'The airport', I told the driver. 'Do you mind if I smoke?'

'Yeah, I mind. There's no smoking.'

I rolled down the window and listened to the wet black tyres hiss through the gentle turns of Campbell Parade.

I didn't want to talk at all, but it's a kind of tax we pay for being human. I pushed my chair to 'recline', leaned back and looked up at the reflections of the scotch on the bulkhead of the Boeing heading for Perth. But I could not avoid listening.

9

'The odd thing is once they go, you know, once the life stops disappearing in front of you and the breathing stops and the machines are taken away and the bed in which they lay once, all eyes…'

Sitting next to me in his pink button-down shirt and ox-blood tasselled loafers.

'…they—the dead, I mean—become just another floating thing to be responsible for in your memory, like where's the bankcard or the keys or the ashtray, and oh! there's Philippa or Willem or Linden or whoever, they're dead… Oh the tropes of memory here in the land of the living…'

He seemed so lucid, too much so for me. Words so sharp you could cut yourself on them. The thing was he looked like someone I knew very well. Someone I'd known at university or who swam at The Icebergs' pool at Bondi or something. Like one of those people who fascinated because they were so cool and never paid you any attention. They just made you self-conscious. A shadow person, an echo-person, a catch-me-fast person.

It had been ten years since I had been to Perth. Ten years since I had last visited my father. Like every city, Perth has its own odour, a scent most distinct during the hours before dawn.

There is salt in the air of course, a nod to the abiding presence of the Indian Ocean. But on certain nights when the breeze blows from the north-east, a more powerful essence soaks the dark air: the ancient memory of the desert. Maybe that's why Dad liked it here. Like the dunes in the deserts of Islam. Peter Weir's film *Gallipoli* rhymes the two deserts well: one eroded and sub-lunar, the other mystical.

I try and make sense of these rhymes between Egypt and Australia—the frangipani would have been familiar, and the flame-trees; the Khamseen wind that behaved like the Fremantle Doctor; the yachts on the Swan and the feluccas on the Nile; the Islamic refrain of *maalesh* and the Aussie's 'she'll be right'; the shared sense of the sacredness of the land, of the land—*al-Khemi*—around the delta-rich Nile, and the Rainbow Serpent crossing the Swan; the fellaheen and the blackfella.

Perth today has an architectural skyline like the punched cards of a computer. It hums with the hubbub of a clamorous and anxious culture about to jettison its innocence. But this July morning, off the plane from Sydney to the hospital, the ancient memory of the desert remains, and it is as if all the gleaming old hotels and banks and shopping centres, the schools and churches, are some dull after-thought.

Going through his flat, sorting out his clothes, there wasn't much to pass on: his small cups for Turkish coffee, his hookah, nargileh, waterpipe, his naturalisation papers signed by Harold Holt, and an 8 x 11 jiffybag, that felt like a sort of MS in the raw. Notes maybe, or studies put together against a book unwritten—recipes—a treatise on the *iskander kebab*?—

dreams. And heavily inscribed on this jiffybag, 'ONLY TO BE OPENED ON MY LAWYER'S INSTRUCTIONS'.

Who was my father really? What sort of man? Wolf or sheep, true or false, sweet or sour? My mother, who took me away to Sydney (at two, three, five finally), claimed he was a gambler, always at a forwarding address. The first sounds I heard—I tell my friends—were the clatter of dice cubes and ice cubes. Between his chef-ness and his cigars he used up all the oxygen in the room, and so was happiest with women who breathed shallowly and aspired only to excellence in the art of devotion.

Kyriakos, an absent father. So to me he became a mythic figure like Dionysius or The Crucified, but done up as Flash Harry, lovable hustler.

'Today', says the doctor, 'forms of masculinity are in crisis. You know all those inner wild man weekends? People trying to figure out from the inside relationships between fathers and sons.'

'Yeah, but I ain't going to no session where they beat up on trees, pound nails, snore loudly and have open mike poetry yelling,' I said. 'Alys doesn't mind. "Just take the garbage on your way out." …I hope, Doc, I don't turn into one of those guys over forty for whom football is more real than women… No, I'm just trying to figure out what sort of man my father was—storyteller, rebel, warrior, trickster, songster, natural gent, man's man, a man born with his boots on, a man born with roses in his mouth—and also to figure out how one dreams oneself together as a man.'

'The normative transitions from youth to maturity have been blocked. Doubly so with you. Write it out, bridge those broken transitions', he said.

So, Toto, I'm trying to connect the dots, pick up the pieces.

10

Born in Cairo, died in Perth. Dreams are back-tracked. I am twenty-nine, alone. After the funeral—he got quite a crowd, mostly old cronies—I caught a bus to Cottesloe, past King's Park, the old brewery by the Swan, back to the familiar dunes of childhood.

On the first bus to Cottesloe it's a clear summer morning in the 1950s, the sort of day that makes your teeth feel clean even if you haven't brushed them. Walking along the road beside the beach I settle on a bench. Early morning sounds of the sleek black crows in the Norfolk pines.

One is for sorrow, two for joy,
Three for a girl, four for a boy,
Five for silver, six for gold,
Seven for a secret ne'er to be told.

The bench was damp and cold, shadowed all morning by the trees, and I slid my notebook under me. Absently, I felt the scars and dents on the bench, familiar as skin.

Watching the sea you begin to love immortal things for an instant. The ocean swelling, with the sun glinting through, then bursting into a long surf slithering from one end of the transit reef to the other. Behind it, another white line forms, then another, and another.

The sparkling ocean of the present slides over my head while I can still smell the bones under. I struck my thigh, half rose, then slowly sank back down again. Soon the sun would reach the bench, and the sands will whiten.

And then: 'How long can you inhabit someone else's tragedy?', announced a voice beside me. 'Telephones are ringing somewhere that we must answer, appointments are made we intend to keep. We're too busy handling our emotional traffic and the sufferings of our neighbours.'

It was him. Pink button-down shirt. Ox-blood tasselled loafers. 'Time untamed will hist for no man', he smiled.

My fingers drummed on my notebook. This guy's weird. He came so quietly I didn't know he was there.

At the edge of the beach the sand burned, the gravelly tar lay afire. Seagulls fell like spots across the eyes. A pregnant woman rearranged her swollen body on a flat rock, the heat rising like a blush.

I closed my eyes, drifting off.

Doctor, I had this dream. Images really. Pulsing like one of those early zoetropes—an official gentleman doffing fez, lady picking up the hem of her skirt, lady flirting fan—images, not still, nor vanishing either. Then I walk across the room and climb through a mirror of a wardrobe to get away from the fatal flickering and enter the baby I used to be. Held by the gloved hands of the midwife who soaks me in my shadows like a photographer rinsing a negative.

Where am I? What am I? Who am I? It feels as though I am minus nine months, nine years, nine lives. Is this like a Writing Cure or a Wiring Cure, Doctor? It's as if a software engineer is trying to get some genetic jingles on the program.

My father in fawn piqué safari jacket with four flap pockets eats pitted dates and reads the paper. A Melbourne Cup special coming up. *The Woman From Tangiers* with Adèle Jergens playing at the refurbished New Grand. Shirley Strickland breaks another athletic record. A white man is beaten with a nulla nulla in Darwin. Kangaroos and dingos are baited with meat cubes and half a gram of strychnine dropped from the air. Migrant men stay in reception camps and health sheds while mothers and children are sent to holding camps at Natham and Cunderdin for six months to Australianise them.

When Violetta leaves Princess Margaret's with her new-born son he'll fatten her up with South African fillet. And if he wins on the horses he'll buy that four-bedroom jarrah bungalow and a Fiat 1500 with alligator bonnet and horizontal vee-shaped grille. They'll go on river excursions and play euchre.

Footprints made their way to her onto the cold emulsion of the foreshore. It was Ox-blood Tasselled Loafers. He turned suddenly. And then something made a bleeding gash on the back of my head. It was so real I had to go and look at myself in the shining hubcap of the '59 Ford Customline to see if I was bleeding.

What do you call it? 'Grief overload'? I wanted to rub the memory from my eyes

Toto, I'm going to write this but I shan't mail it. I smell of salt here.

I have mixed the days. So far apart. Years apart. Yet alike. Yet the same. Maybe it's my several selves that are mixed. Sitting on the cliffs at North Bondi, trying to light a cigarette or on some cerebral ledge way off the planet? Part of you is recovering things that had never taken place; and the other parts are making them happen.

'November 10, 1950. Fine and mild but showers developing later in the afternoon. 73 degrees.'

A man throwing sticks for a dog shatters images in the water. Cottesloe on Kodak Verichrome film—an overchlorinated film, languid, prepsychological. Men with cream flannels fold them into lockers at the Pavilion with their two-tone shoes. They pin keys to their Jantzen trunks, sit in groups around a crystal set listening for news of the Australian Eleven. After a swim they comb Vaseline Hair Tonic through their blueblack hair, while women in royal red satin lastex (featuring the popular quarter skirt) swap Duchess of Sutherland beauty hints.

Perth 1950. Here repressions are slowly surrendered, traditions fought for. Rum and cokes with a chill blast of Presbyterian ozone. We come into the world readymade, fitting categories like a 1950 penny in a banker's groove. Men in grey-green donegals and fawn tweeds pack Four Square tobacco into churchwardens and read Churchill's *Their Finest Hour*. Though Norman Mailer's *The Naked and the Dead* is ninth on the fiction best-seller list. It's twenty-nine flying hours to America (via-English-speaking-countries-all-the-way) on the sleeper-equipped DC6.

It's a Perth of fuel coupons and ex-servicemen. Truman predicts economic recovery. The Big Three discuss Germany. Japan decides between the Asiatic mainland (China, Korea) or US, Britain, France. There's an East-West deadlock on atomic energy control. Tonight, at 8 p.m., the leader of the Opposition, R.G. Menzies, just back from his world tour, broadcasts a policy speech from Victoria, through GWN/WA.

Between the trees I catch sight of my mother, in rayon frock and black and white slung-back toe-peepers, hanging up the washing. On the wireless Rosemary Clooney sings 'Come On-a My House' through a sea of scratches. Violetta adds her voice with a touch of Cairene melisma, a promise of deep impulse behind the cheery exterior.

'You know how long it's been since I heard that song?'

Violetta folding away the clothes in Sydney, arranging them on the bed, talks about Kyriakos to Alys.

'When I married Kyriakos I was eighteen', says Violetta.

'Kyriakos Alexandroglou came to Australia before I was born, in 1926. He left Cairo when he was eighteen and stayed fourteen years till 1940. He was here as a bachelor.'

'In Sydney?'

'All over. Melbourne, Sydney, everywhere. It was in the Depression. He was a blacksheep of the family. But when his sister became widow, Katina, she wrote to him to come over and take over the business and look after her children (she had four kiddies). When his niece, Margarita, married, he decided to leave. Actually the Egyptians made him leave. Over ten years away you cannot get residency in Egypt. He wasn't allowed to stay, so he came back with a re-entry permit, not as a migrant. He stayed six years in Egypt. Every year he used to bribe them, you know, to extend his stay. I came with Yiorgaki in my tummy. I was six months pregnant.'

Violetta's dilemmas as a woman were so complicated. She ended up, at thirty years of age, still living with her parents. This was well after the separation from Kyriakos, the man who saw her as a plump young wife with olive skin who played the piano and spoke five languages.

'What did I need him for? I was eighteen. A convent baby. Bastard just gambling it all away.'

Her eyes are like ankhs with green eyeshadow, and eyebrows like watercolour brushes, her splendid hair thick and hennaed. But her voice has a breakable air, tense and plaintive.

'What did I need with a gambler? That's what I was thinking there in labour. I was scared. All by myself. They hung the little bugger upside down and smacked him, but no reaction. He was in the caul. Smothered in the sac. Then the doctor says, brace yourself, here comes another. And that little bastardo almost killed me.'

'What? Yorgos was a twin?'

'Where was he? Playing manila with those others, no-hopers. Together all the time. *Skata ke to fiari*—shit and the shovel. That's how they were. Never, never there when I needed him.'

Cut from the patterns of light from the Indian Ocean, to the reflections of the rippled turquoise pool at City Beach. Dub in the sound speech m, for the hum of the refrigerator in this empty house in a street where my future wife grew up, just miles from where I played as a child in Cottesloe. The swallows squirting through the air to drink from the pool.

A minute ago heat was rising in shimmering columns and now the wind comes mixed with these strange frequencies, just outside the range of normal apprehension, combining drought crackle and diesel drone. The air is too heavy now to carry the sound right.

Is it the Khamseen, the desert wind, or the Fremantle Doctor? It's whipping up a sandstorm, obliterating the road, a calling card from The Four Horsemen. The sky is a filthy scrim. Human instinct says head away from darkness this absolute. I use my notepad to shield my face. Out of the sand emerge some bastardised International-style housing blocks, slab villas and squat apartment complexes. Buried carcasses of overturned tanker trucks appear on the horizon like mirages, crude oil dripping down the sides.

Am I watching *Mad Max* or is this the road to Baghdad? They're heading for the Jordanian port of Aqaba says the foreign correspondent in camouflage gear. We're on the oil-grey waters in a ship full of refugees in kaffiya and djellabahs. Some nurse wounds, some play backgammon. All of us are escaping the lines drawn in the sand by white colonials.

The man in a red tarboush and worsted abba draws voluptuously on the amber mouthpiece of the hookah with its handsome glass bowl and snake. A woman who wears a frontlet on her forehead of several strings of sequins fitted with each other, forming a broad imbricated surface, like a coat of mail, almost as broad as the palm of her hand, rises to bring him coffee and a sherbet of lemonade. The breeze on the open deck ruffles her blue and white mashla and rattles my nerves like a stick along railings.

Refugees. She consoles her irritable firstborn with Arabic songs. She sends the song through the veins and membranes of the unborn, her lungs pressing onto the soles of the feet. The man picks up the crying kid, a tiny thing in his hands, high above the gunnels of the ship. Is he going to throw him over? The child could fall, fall. Horrible, thrilling. Death might come to us like that. Easy.

I make a slit in my eyes. How many colours are there, doctor, in a field of grass for a crawling baby who has never heard of 'green'? I squeeze my eyelids rapturously together. I am a baby carried through the Hills hoist by my father, damp towels brushing my face, one sock about to fall off my foot. I can see teddy bears with pink umbrellas and blue rainboots surrounded by yellow hearts. Sunlight spills over the back of the bench like a shawl.

An endless shot taken through the centuries. My thoughts have heavy tails which I pursue. Light becomes leaf becomes coal becomes light. Thoughts stare at themselves in candid and placid ways. Milk performs like a frilled dog through hoop after hoop of my guts. Lips, tongue and gums no longer only process food but sound as well. To speak, your tongue unfolds along a libidinal surface, and buds cluster like sunbathers on a beach. There is a clattering morse on a palate, a hammering sound like doors being forced. Eventually reterritorialised as meaning in language. Apple Ball C Duck Elephant F G H Insect Jam K Lemon Mouse N O P Queen Rabbit Sun T U V W X in foX Yacht Zebra.

I pass my hand wearily over my eyes. My notebook bites my thighs. The words *Yiorgos Pun of God* become audible, and as I catch the meaning—so absurd—my body shakes with laughter that's like vomiting.

> Dear Doctor Nemerov,
> It's often like this Doc. I come to the bench for a quiet ponder, and this guy—this Lone Ranger—comes by and impels me to jump up and leave, hugging my notebook, moving my lips as I pace, intently examining the ground. I felt not only Kyriakos there, but also Yiorgos and Manolis. I could smell ancestral things: bad meat and couscous, goats in heat and saltcod. The soul is this? Extraterrestrial swamp gas, bottled in a body? Can the ground drink up what history has spilled? Doc.?
> I'll mail this now. It will give me something to do. You could write just a postcard, one sentence, to give me a diagnosis. Anything on a postcard sounds like an epigram.

I head for the Post Office to post my letters and find a note from Zoë inviting me to a *'Come-As-You-Aren't' pre-Biennale party. Mystery Cocktails!* A blue and white letter from Libby and Stewart from their Greek island. A postcard from the doctor in red ink. A re-addressed letter from the sub-titling department wanting an update on the Kastellorizo project.

On past the Space Invader video arcade. A pimply kid with *Machine Head* printed on his T-shirt. I think of Toto's boyfriend Shake. In Kuwait they would be holding M-16s. He plays *Missile Command*, the screen throbbing with insect-like skulls, geometric killer-spikes. To finish with a brief dirge and the words THE END flashing over a mushroom cloud before being swallowed.

I throw the mail onto the passenger seat and glide the Humber around the elegant crescents of City Beach. Here Alys grew up in the heathland never cramped by shoes. I picture her, Toto's age, in whimsical candystripes amongst the pearl-blue salt bush and the flowery spikes of the grass tree. Her brothers catching dugites, bob-tailed lizards and whipsnakes. En famille on Rottnest, the boats rocking in Geordie Bay, the wind teasing the calm waters of the anchorage into thin waves that snap out their brief lives on the shoreline.

I park the car not far from the ocean. I picture Alys as she is now in that sea of pussy-willows dancing in a blonde heat. Everywhere in my life there are pre-figurations of love. The seemingly random events of life form patterns. These patterns change, re-form all the time. But they are always the same under the surface. *To have contemplated human life for forty years is the same as to have contemplated it for ten thousand years. For what more wilt thou see?* Pippa, Kate, Deirdre, Zoë, Alys—a broken chain. The women who save me but lay bare a kind of Oedipal disaster. Screen-ladies, like those in Dante's *Vita Nuova*. There were glimpses in Glebe, in Liss, Bannister, the East Village, Pula, Rhodos, Marrakesh. We had loved each other before we had known each other. Been unfaithful to each other before we met. *We go on loving,* says Violette Le Duc, *those we have loved in other forms, or else we begin to cherish in other forms those we have cherished in the past. Nothing changes. Everything gets transformed.*

By three, the sea retreats at low tide to great distances. I take out a cigarette and let the wind unravel the smoke from my mouth and nostrils. Mist is the veil between one world and another. Mum and Dad are away off arguing. I can't tell them apart. They go into the water and disappear into the dark lines, the meadows of sea grass and ribbon weed.

The limestone reefs with fissures in them like mouths half-covered in grey-golden beards. Hollow in places making the ground itself a sounding board.

I'm watching the movie of my life: Kyriakos and Violetta. Paul Henreid and Bette Davis: stateless war refugees, the deck of a freighter. He lights two cigarettes at a time, passes one to her. A repeated ritual, symbol of doomed love.

This theme, the divorce of my parents, I am forced to repeat or devise variations upon exhaustingly, so that I exhaust its meaning, and myself.

Once upon a time, they lived happily ever after. Except for that divorce thing.

I see a red-necked stint that has migrated from Siberia. My hand goes out for the postcard. I cannot find my glasses. The message is written in red. I fold the postcard into a paper boat and find myself up to my knees in the Indian Ocean holding a real boat with the Greek word *Metafora* on it, and my fingernails painted with red nail polish. What does the note say?

You have fallen into art. Return to life.
Doc.

12

It was Friday morning. The alarm clock rolled little 7, 0, and 0 cards over the 6, 5 and 9, red on black. Elizabeth, Liz, Lizzy, Beth, Betty, Lotte, Totty, Toto woke and went to the thin balcony three stories up near the southern end of Bondi Beach. She looked down at the lane which did a dog-leg off Lamrock and the stagey rippled turquoise of Campbell Parade. There was no view of the surf from here, just a tall tatty palm tree and a rear view of the apartments opposite and the pock-marked stretch of macadam where Shake sometimes did deals in cheap reefers with the skateboarders under the frangipani.

Toto at twelve was anxious, was radiant, was excitingly mutable. At twelve she was a charter member of a generation that had a special way of laughing, of talking and ordering priorities. She and her friends—boyz and grrls—had a way of encoding everything from song lyrics to orange vinyl hand-bags. On weekends, she dressed, according to her father, like an expensive cartoon; on schooldays she rolled up the waist-band to make the pleated skirt short. At twelve she was waiting desperately for adult life to begin.

What would she do today? Alys was at Zoë's for the day, helping with her installation for the Art Gallery of New South Wales. It was a hot one already and the southerly sucked through the cracks in the stucco. On weekends the wind carried some Afro-Latin music from the Bondi Pavilion, slan-ting it across the bay to arrive in distorted shelves of sound, along with the mentholated resin of gum trees. Right now the soundtrack was untended car alarms and washing cracking in the wind. What would she do? School or skip?

Shake, a sixteen-year-old, and Toto's current 'crush object' could be at the Pavilion already, maybe from the night before. Shake was his *nom de street*, as trader in the powdery leaf—"shake"—that came off the marijuana plant that he sold in loose joints. The heads he kept for private consumption. Shake—real name Mitchell—had fled a predacious family to live off his wits in a boarding house on Consett Street. He had heartbreaking eyes and hair the colour of a leather jacket. Hope and trust had been ripped out like cables, but Toto believed that love could heal all.

When George and Alys were introduced to him they were not too sure of the T-shirt that went to his ankles with PURE SEX written on it. Or the tattoo high on the shoulder that had *S.O.S.* on it. 'Save Our Souls?' asked Alys. "Nup. 'Same Old Shit'," said Shake.

'He doesn't ride herd', offered Toto.

Up to the tricky terrain of pubescence Toto's father had kept a kind of benign negligence. When she was all surprise and fluff like a young duck, he nodded gravely on the sidelines as Alys counted the teeth she cut, and the knees she bruised, and the tears she wept for the cold dead fledgling on the pavement; or when she refused to weep in a thunderstorm, he nodded gravely, and he hugged her.

Now she was becoming a lank anatomy, all leg and hair and stare like a young colt. Now strange spasms of indolence would keep her inside for days looking at herself in the mirror.

The one in the bedroom had a good reflection with a fine degree of loss. She'd fluff her spiky fringe at the front, transforming the angles of her face, pointing up the slant of her eyes into which she would stare, stare.

Still, 'normal', as Alys pointed out, wasn't Dad's particular area of expertise, personally or professionally. 'He wouldn't know normal if it bit him on the behind.'

But Dad insisted he knew the world of adolescent males. Shake was living the quivering sullen city of sixteen-year-olds, with its long rambling walks to the empty arcades smelling of popcorn, frying oil and urine, the surreptitious whisky in polystyrene cups, the XX-rated porn flick signs in doorways, the wild dogs dragging leashes, the incomprehensible yearning that began to fix itself on the person of Toto and her cheeks illuminated by cinematic love as big as a football field.

Toto headed downstairs with her towel over her shoulder. The door opened on a blast furnace. As she walked she let the blandishments of this Indian summer sun beat down on her bare arms. She kept her head down. Her innocence was disconcerted easily by the uncompromising light. Cracks would appear in the pavement of her being and she had to drive her self-consciousness inward or else it would take hold of her every step. She kept her head down. Being twelve, everything got magnified and distorted. Being a girl, you were never allowed to be in charge.

The silver-grey coastal trees—dwarf bottle-brush and white oleander—vibrated with the high pitch of the cicada. They stopped abruptly as she skipped by. A silence ballooned up suddenly underscoring this plateau before the rush hour. Soon commuters and schoolkids would be filing into buses, passing through the iron curtain of subway trains and into the artificial tunnels. Out here time would float for a brief moment and conjure the footprintless stretch of coast it must have been for the Aborigines among the tea-trees and Banksia.

From the top of the park she could see a knot of people, and Shake, in his striped denim flares, shirt off, sleek-skinned, with his mates.

Toto felt a languor, a torpor dragging on her body like a molestation. The centre of her being felt the wave-front of ordinary existence as pressure and density. She couldn't handle him right now. She'd go and pick up the mail from the post office and walk behind the Pavilion and swim at the northern end of the beach. The waves were manageable there between the flags and she could disappear in the mercury glitter of wash and seaspray under the morning sun. She would doze on the Pacific slept by the waves, the length of her young body bobbing afloat, like a cork.

After the swim Toto buried her face in the salty crook of her arm. The sun beat down from a flawless sky in velvety waves. The breeze from the beach breathed along the down of her legs and the back of her neck. It also blew the pages of her father's blue airmail pages across the sand. As she turned around quickly, she saw Shake. He had an unlit cigarette over his ear and he said,

'You wanna wag?'

'No, I don't wanna wag.'

'Yeah, whatever.'
He then turned round and called a friend,
'Hey Curtis, wait up.'
And was gone.

13

Dearest Toto... Feeling uneasy here in this distinguished house with its coat-of-arms, oaken furniture soaked in expensive tobacco and wines, its oval portraits of stalwart descendants. I'm a supine detective trying to piece together details of my father's life, who died broke after dissipating three fortunes by sheer joyful improvidence. My father left no inheritance, took out no insurance. By chance there was enough money for the funeral. There was none of the middle class instinct for forward planning and the managerial view of life. But are we sure they'll save us?

For the capitalist wants a guarantee his tomb will be ready to receive him after he dies. But why this eagerness to be in stone? What combination of egoism and necrophilia is there in that mind-set that wants to kiss its own grave? George wondered if putting writing into a book was a bit like that too. Remember, Yiorgaki, Dad cherished his breath, not his death. *It comes easy, goes easy* was his signature song.

La vita o si vive o si scrive said Pirandello. Even the very best writing invariably kills the greatest and most intimate part of any experience that it seeks to express. Being dead's a drag. Writing is embalming the dead. All the volumes of Proust could not match a twenty-minute breakfast on a spring morning at Memento's at Bronte Beach. The more restlessly I try and encode these shimmying experiences, the more profoundly the writing obliterates the immediacy of memory.

This 'novel' I am constantly writing is always the same bloody one. And it might be described as a variously sliced up or torn apart book of the self. A belated identification this, torn up and across like letters into irreconcilable halves, quarters, sixteenths.

My old man was a businessman but without the killer instinct. You see that propensity in some of the relations, the richer tribal families. As a gambler I see my father making Karamazovian bargains with destiny, breathtakingly rich one day, borrowing $20 the next. Incongruity is man's recognition of chaos. But did he really have a nose for the abyss, and did I inherit this nihilism? Some say gambling is a continual suicide; that it kills time because there is no past, no significant future, just living in an eternal and optimistic present tense.

One day he would woo noble women in a tux, a beau monde he conjured where all the telephones were white; the next he was in a singlet among hoods, bookmakers and ex-jockeys. He hobnobbed with the quality at the roulette wheel, but was clearly a sucker for the *maudits*. A winner and a loser both, the whole catastrophe.

This was before young Violetta with her embonpoint and her dowry. The sideways matriarchal networking of *proxenia* by gossip and calculated financial settlements allowed the eighteen-year-old convent girl to be matched with the seasoned forty-year-old. My mother's mother was Greek, but my mother's father was Sicilian, from Santa Lucia del Mela, 40 klicks from Messina, where Italy kicks Sicily into the Mediterranean. But they were all part of the cosmopolitan, hedonistic, intermarried melange of Egypt's pre-Nasser European community.

But meanwhile at the other end of the world Viola was having to change addresses fourteen times in three years— furnished rooms, the houses of relatives, squalid apartments. The rootlessness was driving her crazy. So by the time her brothers and parents arrived and settled in Sydney she was ready to go there to them with me, Yiorgaki.

Ten years later, after growing up in Sydney with my mother's extended family, the court allowed visits to Perth. From then on I'd go to visit Dad every summer.

I'll never forget the first.

I was picked up at the airport by Dad and two friends. They were unshaven, but not my father who wore English suits and Italian shoes and smoked Cuban cigars. Together they looked like villains out of the hard-boiled dick cheese 1950s of the Mike Hammer era, terminal greasers in a Ford Customline full of dashboard rembetika.

Gunning the car they made me realise for the first time that the internal combustion engine was a contained explosion. The conversation was Greek *manga*, a hepcat jive talk that went over my crewcut. The sound quality of the music was chthonic, as though a 45 had been scored by a nail file. There was so much bass the centre of gravity was way down in the axles. But the bouzouki—a kind of alternate-universe guitar—sketched out a get down dirty blues as tough as marram-grass.

And instead of arriving at some suburban-bourgeois home under the tyranny of 'tidiness', we arrived in a kind of warehouse. A dim-lit largish space with no divisions between bedroom, loungeroom and kitchen. There was a double bed and a couch and a campbed. On the gas ring a man put on an ibriki, a tiny copper pot with a long handle, and made coffee as black as Kuwaiti crude. The transistor continued some raggedy-arsed country honk and the men sat down to play manila.

They offered semolina cake while I layabed under a blanket of topcoats and jackets. I fell asleep to the mind-bending supertwang of the kleftiko music, a distant cousin to those variations on 'Louie, Louie' and 'Tequila', as the men slapped down cards and hissed through their stubble.

For years when I'd visit Dad in Perth, or meet him halfway in Melbourne, he'd establish rendezvous at shady gambling halls guarded by burly bouncers with ouzo and basil on their breath.

He stood out with his cut-throat dago looks, a North African fez-wearing mulatto in pin-striped suit. They would greet him with a 'Yiassou, Farouk' or a 'Salaam-alaykum'.

We'd play snooker, in the dreamy underwater feel of bright lights on green baize in those down-at-heel Hellenic clubs. Dad gut-heavy and slow moving dissecting rack after rack. Balls flying in off the break and the cue balls on sonar, charting order through random table patterns. Six ball slowly down the end rail—plop. Seven straight in the side. Etc. Santo and Johnny on the jube. Sleepwalk pool. Me idly holding the bridge. Partagas cigar, smell of aniseed and pimento.

There was a restaurant he ran in Sydney, Pitt Street, when the place became a kind of Cucina Nostra, cut off from the public, where rackets and races were discussed. Mobsters eating lobsters. And jokes would fly:

'Hey, Kyriakos, it tastes like dishwater.'

'Needs more soap?'

'Hey, Kyriakos, I'm going to pizzas.'

'Hey, Kyriakos, what's this? Unidentified Frying Object.'

Their girlfriends, all teased-hair and glossy pantsuits, put on lipstick and took them to Holiday Inn Ballrooms with vinyl wallpaper. Father was magnanimous, fanning high-denomination bills in his big hands.

'You made me love you ... you woke me up to do it...'

'Hey, Kyriakos...'

I've been a sucker for the lowlife ever since, in every city's redlight district, with its mondo bongo music or boom-titty-boom drum solos. And as soon as I left home at eighteen I cruised this landcape strewn with pizza crusts and gin flasks; the world of stubble and unsettling smells on the fingers that next morning could never quite be placed.

'Is it easier to wipe out the world than save its problems?', my mother would ask, as mothers do. 'You men never deal with your problems until it's too late. You like your gratification straightaway.'

Did I really want to end up with all those depressives on the fringe, the clubby males afraid of social contact, the failures at love and work? Is this true? The world has a use-by date; now the universe is not so healthy and forgiving. My life has been, like my father's, a rollercoaster of procrastination and crisis. Like all of humanity we've been living with deficit and on credit.

Back in Sydney I put away what he left me, and the jiffybag, in the iron-safe in my office. I had bought the safe second-hand. I had a few first editions in there as well—*The Balcony of Europe, Journal of the Fictive Life, The Man Who Made Friends With Himself*—and a bottle of ouzo. I waited for instructions from the notary.

The day after my father's funeral, I'm travelling in the Humber along the coast road from Swanbourne to Scarborough and Trigg. I used to trawl those dunes and empty streets: bits of past life appear, reappear, as though it were the same, unchanging. Except maybe the OTC masts and microwave towers. But the rolling sine curves of the dunes, the stroke of the cicadas, the dogged little shrubs fighting against brine and shifting sands: nothing changes, everything is transformed.

One event stands out from this, going through my father's possessions. There were some photos taken back in 1964 at Cottesloe beach. I'm standing on my father's shoulders, flexing my muscles for the camera. An icon of patriarchy and masculinity—'the Arnold Schwarzenegger feeling'—a hard-on everywhere. A Mediterranean tradition, too, of never leaving adolescence because it is the time during which you become a man. Forgivable, this evidence of pre-teen narcissism.

Embarrassed by the evidence of that cruel little god so despised by my women friends I decided almost without thinking to tear them up. Then I decided to keep them.

Tearing, splitting: one half seen, the other seeing. There is always a fork in the road on the way to ourselves.

Still what I value from all this is the lack of seriousness that made all stereotypes look grim. He put a spin on the capitalist instinct, real estate, class codes, landlords and language. And for that I love him.

A few days pass trying to get on to a member of the Castellorizian Club for an interview. Like so much else, connections fray. We measure out our lives with Beep-to-Beep calls.

BEEP. Hello, Yiannis. This is George. I'm calling to get your friend, the Cassie historian, Perry's phone number. Please get back to me.

BEEP. Hi, George, it's Yiannis. Perry's number is 667 3300, I'll be speaking to you...

BEEP. Hi Perry, this is George. Do you remember me? We met at Yiannis's party. If you remember give me a call. My number is 365 6482.

BEEP. Hi, George. This is Perry. I'm sorry it took so long to return your call, but I accidentally erased your phone number and had to call John to get it. Bye.

BEEP. Hi, Perry. No need to apologise. I wasn't sure if you remembered who I was. I'll be home tonight.

BEEP. Hi George, it's Perry. I was away on business for a few days. Yes I remember you. You're writing a book. Bye now.

BEEP. Hi Perry, sorry I didn't get back to you sooner. I was out of, well, town.

BEEP. Hi George, it's Perry. I'm returning your call... Bye.

BEEP. Hi, Perry, this is George. Listen this is getting absurd. I was wondering if you'd like to have lunch this Monday? Or if lunch isn't your thing we could meet in the evening at my place.

BEEP. Hi George. This is getting funny. It's Perry and it's 6:30. I'm afraid tomorrow lunch is not good for me, but give me a call back and we'll schedule another time. Speak to you later.

Aha! it's only 6:50! He's still home—I'll call him.

Hi. This is Perry. I'm not in now, but please leave your name and number and remember to wait for the beep...

Perry! It's, me! George! Hello! Hello! Perry! If you're home pick up the phone! You just called me! You can't be out already. This is incredible. PERRY, I'M HERE! PERRY!

I open the blue and white aerogramme from Libby:

> ...today we walked to a beach, or perhaps more accurately an outlet onto the sea, through fields of red poppies, terraces of olive trees. down we walked from the Plaka & Castro which are high on a fortified mountain peak & as we got further away they took on a weird perspective; the silence and stillness of the landscape give it a special quality. it's very harsh in the midday sun, even hostile. when we go to the beach we found old mining equipment & a warehouse—to extract the sulphur in the rock. & some small weekenders, fishing sheds. at 1st no signs of people but later discovered an old man & a younger one preparing to go out fishing. near the warehouse we looked down cliffs into the water, which was very deep and swelling against the rocks. further along great chunks of rock met the sea—there was something about it, too vast for the human scale. I thought what it would be like to swim down there, a bit terrifying. there are other parts of the island like this, more or less impossible to walk along because the cliffs plunge into the sea.

a local eccentric spends all his time unravelling a ball of string as he walks about the streets—an all-consuming obsession. there's also a mad boy around 15 who bellows like a cow & walks around town alone, eyes rolling, ignored by all, but free to go where he wants at least. we had just finished a meal out in the open & there was slice of bread left in the basket—he was walking by at the time & came up suddenly, snatched the bread & ran off. weird. we see him outside the souvlaki bar, hungry. there's no market, no cinema, but the shops are pleasant & it's interesting to see what new vegetables appear now and then. at first—tomatoes, peppers, aubergines—but since, we've seen marrow, beans, okra, cabbage, cauliflower etc.

A trip to Greece would be nice. But I was travelling inside. I was my own foreign country.

Violetta, dashing out her coffee dregs in the backyard, used to say character is everything, circumstances don't count. You can break with people and places. You can change your situation, but into each situation you carry your torment with you and often discover you've merely added remorse to regrets.

That night I had a dream that I had come home to Sydney to find all the lights on and understood immediately that she had come back. And I went from one room to another calling out loud. I had been smoking quite a bit and I went everywhere in the house, then stood outside the bedroom before the closed door, and I knew they were inside.

15

Zoë tilts back in the chair and looks at Alys in a detached appraising look, after the melting look of a moment ago.

Lovemaking with Zoë—so brilliant, so plotless, yet never meandering or thin—had left Alys a little dazed and surprised at her own body's collaboration. What drove her limbs and her senses seemed carved out of a powerful substance, from a darkness deep inside where everything shuddered.

Zoë looking like a bored but confident courtesan, her slender fingers curving around the cigarette. 'Nice weather for a sultry adultery', she joked. 'I badly wanted you to come to tell you I wasn't cooking up any sexual conspiracy. I know some people like planning and scheming more than fucking. It doesn't just run along gender lines either.'

Alys' smile was crooked-serene, the two sides of her self wavering between consent and refusal at first, and then later torn by more primal ebbs and flows that mixed contempt and love. O jesus yes no yes no. She got dizzy, even a little sick. But they couldn't stop kissing, engulfed by an irresistible force that took everything with it: the bed, the fridge, George and the job, the dull inert things and the cold hard facts. Alys slipped free of it all.

Why do we do what we do? The desires of the heart are as crooked as corkscrews, the poet said. Our motivations come in clusters: egotism? altruism? domination? submission? scepticism? animal faith? Who knows.

'It's fantasy land', said Alys looking at the array of costumes and sets in the loft. 'Why do I always feel motel-lust here?'

82

She recalled the afternoons she pretended to be Zoë. A person who took her life in long strides, who set herself goals, then fleshed them out. While she, working as a fact-checker for magazines, was always bartering with reality, trying to cut a better deal. Sitting at Zoë's kitchen table alone, in jealous absorption, the studio was there to teach her. Her very dreams seemed a kind of show Zoë put on for her. And then when she cut her long, very long hair short like Zoë's, she performed an ecstatic unravelling dance over the cropped plait and bundles laid out on butcher's paper. George was flabbergasted but managed to retrieve the situation by saying how he liked the way the hair sleeved out fine at the nape.

There was the rattle of glasses and ice. Zoë laid hold of the neck of a Chianti bottle and put it between her legs. Adroitly she heaved upon it—oooh!—shaking her breasts, pulling the cork with a how's that? flourish.

Alys wondered what next. The act had been achieved, the prize won. She felt something in her spirit had been forfeited. They needed somehow to talk about George, George who was once so pure and fresh and happy in both their lives, but now was so troubled, like a house that had been burgled, like a cock fresh out of sunrises.

'Poor little chook' Alys called him. 'Poor little specimen.' That was paying him back for the way he said 'my' wife, like he said 'my' car, 'my' career.

Zoë and Alys embraced. Alys asked, 'What about the wine?'

'It's breathing.'

'That makes one of us.'

They laughed. Alys plagiarised Zoë's laugh which seemed to bounce off the cave in the back of her throat. Was it a form of respect or parody? Awkwardly Alys began to talk about George's videolepsy.

'When George couldn't sleep for months I made an outpatients appointment at a big general hospital', began Alys. 'He was given thorough-going physical examinations by the head of the unit whose clinic he was attending: from gavels on knees to electrodes on the scalp. I listed food intake, booze, history with drugs. We waited in specialists' rooms all chrome and glass like some postmodern airport lounge, or else dolled up like regional motel rooms.'

'Yeah, I know. Those rooms that look like they've been decorated by Elvis or the hostess on "The Wheel of Fortune".'

'Indian files of locums gawked, questioned him—poor little chook—and disappeared. Nurses took litres of blood. The head of the unit shrugged his shoulders. Therapists were recommended. They proceeded to track down hysterical symptoms through the swamplands of George's mind. George, of course, thought all this a "flako West Coast bullshit trip". He said it was only the job. Work was a pressure cooker of adrenalin, caffeine and power plays. But plausible aetiologies were traced. I mean the guy's not exactly Oprah Winfrey material, but—absent father, loopy mother, crazy mixed up nationalities, only child. His loneliness as a child was populated with fascinating and threatening third persons. And on top of all that a series of failed relationships, failed attempts at fiction.'

'Well', added Zoë, 'absence of the father brings with it a fantasy that you can make yourself up. Lacking an effective rival this only son becomes his own rival. But what gets him into trouble is his Levantine insistence upon a life of infinite possibilities. He thinks he's in the fucking *One Thousand and*

One Nights. So going out on a particular night, he'd say it was a night when lovers will be united in the moonlight forever, or they may perish horribly. Because that night wasn't a date on the calendar but a break in the sequence of time. I mean it's what attracted me to him in the first place. With him the ordinary could be invaded by the unexpected. That he believed, *really* believed, that our fate hangs by a thread. That salvation comes by whim or accident. That things were opposite not in meaning, but in time. That time was like a tape that could whizz back an inch or two on its reel; that yes and no could ride the same sentence in the same breath.'

'Like *uh-huh* meaning yes and no?'

'Or like the way that married couples can be strangers', Zoë said, pursing her mouth and tilting the head sardonically.

'Yes', affirmed Alys, looking into Zoë's green eyes, a green beyond the smart green of the paintbox, a mix of jungle-green and seagreen, hues that changed with the light.

'That the world', went on Zoë, 'might be permeable, mutable, destructible, as in the *Arabian Nights*. You know? That you could pull space or time apart like a curtain to reveal a parallel existence. What was it that Pasolini said? That the truth lies in several dreams, not just the one.'

'So what about George and you?'

Alys had felt hostage to these previous lives, previous landscapes, that pre-dated her, of which she knew only morsels, without true substance. Her imagination had embroidered fantasies from photos and letters George had left carelessly, or carefully? around.

'George and me?'

'Didn't he take you off Rory Butcher? Tell me. Tell me all there is to tell.'

'I'll tell you all if you arrange yourself into this pose for me. I need an extra body on the third panel of the folding screen.'

16

'It has to look like this', she said, showing her a puzzling scene in an old Dutch painting. The neck was craned in a submissive gesture, in what looked an uncomfortable position. The folds of the drapery formed surrogate body parts, extra breasts and vaginas. The face had the withdrawn look of a puppet.

Zoë set up the scenario and adjusted the tripod and camera and began to speak of this early time. A time, thought Alys, *before* Alys, before Toto, before swollen ankles, before life had become overwhelmed by domestic detail, dissolving into a Mum-and-Dad sandmoving combine. Before George and the compromised jobs which had seemed more reliable than art, because less psychically demanding. Hadn't that backfired!

Alys watched Zoë move around some Besser bricks, which threw into prominence some fundamental attribute of sex. Alys admired her ability to wield power like a man; admired the way she didn't preach equality, just wanted things evenly matched. But she lived in another country, of which those with kids were expatriates.

The looking glass was tilted up and pouring on Alys a light that seemed to fix her, with the clouds behind her like silver meringues. Everything inside the frame became more hieroglyphic, the kilim, the vase of tiger lilies, even the legs of the couch. Alys craned her neck, naked, attentive.

Zoë talked of her early days with the painter Rory Butcher in Chechaouen when they lived high over a valley in Morocco. She spoke in a flat way but told it well.

Of the time twenty years ago when George was young and pure and happy. When he shambled after people who interested him like Rory and Zoë. It was his Kerouac phase: you know, mad to live, mad to talk, mad to be saved, all at the same time with nothing to do but combust.

Zoë was a not very serious photographer then. She took shots of backgrounds, absences. Rory Butcher was the very very serious painter. An abstract expressionist who produced heavy webbings of paint on an aggressive scale. They were like maps of journeys, like the unravelling shape of a ship's wake or the flow of rush hour traffic or the tangled arteries of interstate ramps. 'Mondrian on a subway rattler', said the critic of the *New York Times*. Obsessive, compelling forms were constantly being tested in the huge winter studio of Chechaouen, a mountain retreat in the Rif, overlooking olive and cactus. Rory was drawn to the colours—astonishing blues, corals and reds, deep greens the colour of Easter eggs, and the rich ambers of the Morisco rooftops. He was also drawn to the small polyglot community of country-hoppers and carpetbaggers around the Hotel Andaluz, and they were drawn to him. They'd seen it all, the trade offs, the briberies, the coups, the civil wars, even executions. They'd seen it all with an infuriating stateless indifference.

There was a history of it at the place, founded in the fifteenth century by the refugees from Spain, regarded as Moors by the Spaniards, Europeans by the Moors. It was the next big place after Ketama at the foot of the Rif, hustler headquarters of the hash trade, where cars were customised to carry bricks of hashish past roadblocks, through the backroads to the isolated fishing villages of El-Jebha or Torres de Alcala, and out to Europe.

Zoë closed her eyes. Sighed. Went on.

Rory was a big man with a complexion the colour of a pastry cook. He would threaten both men and women. To women he signalled his availability, despite Zoë. He let them know that he found them exciting, but that danger lurked if they were alone. He was part of that generation of male artists who, like GIs in a sex-war, decided that the country couldn't be won, so it had to be destroyed.

To men the challenge was not to bore or bullshit him. He had this knack of humiliating you for lacking conviction. Rory had it all. Talent, money, humour, looks. He had it all. Just a bit too perfect and arrogant. He lacked humility. He needed a comeuppance.

By the time George arrived Rory couldn't tell if he was up or down. He was both at the same time and so he got stuck, permanently, in a downward spiral. The paintings that began as journeys seemed to isolate him like the end of a corridor. Rory used to beat Zoë up as a kind of post-sex purgative. They would shower then head down to the tiled lobby of Hotel Andaluz, drink mint tea at the terrace tables or play cards in the patio of the courtyard. Nobody said anything about the bruises.

Over another wine Alys considered this woman with the staunch ability to withstand disaster. She listened to the voice, now lowered, furring the notes, now gaining steadiness and edgier harmonies. Having to tell the story from the past clashed with her hard won *carpe diem* feeling that Life is Now.

George had been travelling rough. Staying in basic hotel rooms *sans douche*, you know, retirement homes for fleas. Hassled by those self-adhering cockroaches called guides. He was young, and his skin glowed, you know? From a fellow traveller he kept a copy of a *Tits and Ass* magazine to pacify the pasha-shaped wardens who timelessly front the registration desks of these places and who seem given to unpredictable fits of pique.

One night Rory, drunker than he knew, huge eyes sliding in gleaming fluids like primitive marine animals, fixed them on George, a travelling Aussie. Then fixed them on the bottle of brandy by his elbow. They drank, they argued. George the writer, Rory the painter. They headed for the studio together. Up the stairs Rory was fulminating about critics and academics and institutions issuing salary cheques, accumulating credits and diplomas out of the human blood spilt on the other side of the planet ... on and on.

In the studio there was the smell of linseed oil and turps. The walls were covered with stretchers, gouaches, unstretched oils. There was a high swivel stool and easel. On a long trestle table a mess of paint cans, tubes and brushes, and dinner plates used to mix colours. There were Rory's massive shoes Pollocked with drips.

'This was where the hippie travellers would be asked to strip and model. I would come in and the model's bottom would disappear into the bedroom, with Rory's charcoal finger marks all over it.'

George and Rory got on well. Rory, his mouth displaying the ferocious chew-hold his teeth had upon a big cigar, reminded George of his father. Though Rory had a big dog pathos as well that George could see through, a kind of astral baby at the core. A liquefying Camembert. George on the other hand was more your avocado. Tough hide, softer in the middle, but suffering had given him something more solid at the centre.

Everyone senses that, especially if you try and put the squeeze on him.

Doctor Nemerov unfolded the letter from Perth and read,

Caro dottore,

Re: Writing Cure. I'm experimenting. I can write, *There is no Doctor Nemerov, no detective, no Bones the cat,* and feel strangely relieved. Then I feel an aching loss. You the Doctor, Belacqua the detective, and even the cat are all part of this life I've precipitated on paper; part of you remain with me. 'You' are both my urge for collective experience and a function of how I think about myself. So, Doc, it's a compromised redemption this writing business, a failed gospel.

You do not exist before this word, you. (Three letters, *y-o-u*.) Jumpstarted by it, you are what happens while performing the signs and passwords of the text.

Let us suppose a smart white overcoat is given you. Then I must invent a peg to hang it from, keys to look for, absent trousers in which to have left them, then a sun to light the street. It's exhausting. As you walk along the pavement the new building opposite in its shift of light and shadow seems as fitful as a moth. The cooling mechanism of an airhammer whines in your ears. It just about bakes a hole in your skull. The jackhammers underfoot thump you like an engine in the body of a caique. You pick up the vibes through the soles of your shoes, and then the concrete slabs buckle underfoot, the telegraph poles tilt forward and cars slide to the foot of the hill. Before long rooftiles, striped couches, wooden stairs, old bathtubs with claw feet follow you down the black hole of a full stop.

The problem with writing is the split I feel about living my life inside the twenty-six letters of the alphabet and the contrary desire to be a real body in real space. The desire to dissolve the self into language, to become words, artefact, book; and the desire to peel the layers back to find something unmediated, unlearned, alive.

Could the fracture of the keys, those little rounded squares of the keyboard, put Humpty Dumpty together again?

The Doctor tore off a page from his prescription pad, uncapped his pen, and wrote on the back: *A hyphen might.*

18

Alys looked at Zoë's eyes, wide apart. An hypnotic look, or a hypnotised one. Zoë touched Alys' skin. Felt the pulp and bones of another's hand. Touch. What's it mean? It doesn't mean anything. The body doesn't give signs; it gives itself in the circuits of blood like the slow raking of pebbles along a beach.

Zoë continued the story. They'd talk past each other, tenderness badly awry, Rory skidding suddenly into violence, Zoë like a woman in a parachute waiting for it to open. Always resentful, Rory's regular ploy was to refuse to speak, to humiliate her into admitting she needed the relationship by speaking first.

Exhausted by the Punch and Judy, Zoë retreated into the silence of the darkroom. It was photography that kept her going. Staring into the viewfinder left her empty. From that emptiness she could pirate calm; she'd seek out the f-stop, where her joy and terror ran power off the same circuit. These were like instamatic poems: incomplete, often shrouded in fog like eggwhite, pointing to some other strange world, just out of reach of understanding or information. Then, in the bathroom turned darkroom, playing with the process chemicals at the wet bench, watching the properties of eroding nitrates, seeing the images decompose into blurry stains. She loved their half-life between representation and matter, and she was having a small success, the promise of a show in New York. Rory resented it. There could only be one artist in his kingdom. But he also resented his own success, the work was being corporatised and museumised.

George, meanwhile, had moved into a studio room in the mountain retreat. They gravitated to each other. The last thing Zoë needed: fresh complications, reawakening muscles of the heart that had been paralysed for so long. But when Rory flew to London for a show, they talked, smoked, the glasses ebbed, the shadows inched, knees went weak and hearts thumped in throats. Zoë was attracted to George's grave hardness sitting awkwardly on his youthfulness. For George maybe it was just more sex on the road, the lines of demarcation blurring between love and the purely physical response to Zoë's peach-coloured bikini panties that stretched across her lovely bottom.

Alys thought of George and Zoë lying naked side by side. Like attracts like?

In that spring, when heat drew unsettling desires out of the ground in scented columns of sap, invading the senses, George had marked Zoë, physically, psychically. He patterned her desire to his rhythm. One rhythm set off a rambling purr in her throat, another rhythm produced screams and repeated cries. Unplanned, a phenomenon of nature, like the North African sunlight frothing over the newly budded leaves with points of light. And Rory? By summer he had killed himself.

When Rory found out they had run off together, he didn't follow. He just spat, *Bitch! Without her I'm dead, but I hate her.* He stayed behind in Chechaouen. For a few weeks he wasted himself on drink and one-night stands, ending up alone after a day alone in his studio. Colour drained from his canvases—just a poisonous green, slate grey, putty. On his last day he stared at a half-finished canvas, dementedly aware of being alone in the building. He loosened the tacks and stripped the canvas away from its stretcher and dug his heels into the thick and sticky paint smearing the colours in a flux of emotion.

Then, suddenly, he raged against the long-time domestics, Abdul and Mohammed. He accused them of stealing from the fridge hearts meant for the cats. He rigged up a gun in the fridge, triggered to go off when the door opened. He started drinking. The short summer darkness slipped by in a few hours. The light returned after the whiskey night; the tight testy tenor of Bob Dylan wavered along its druggy slopes, accusingly: *Whatever you wanted, what can it be? Did somebody tell you you could get it from me? Is the scenery changing? Am I getting it wrong? Is the whole thing going backwards? Are they playing our song?*

The moments out of register. 'In the brain', Rory used to say, 'a mere millimetre can mean hundreds of miles'. The cat closed her eyes and settled into the neat bundle of her body before her empty dish. As she yawned, her head disappearing behind its pale pink mouth, *Bang!* They found him in the sticky black pudding of his own blood.

In his will Rory Butcher left Zoë Ashford a Moroccan coin—a mere dirham—minted in the year 1975, the year they met. The story with a full front page photo of Zoë appeared in the *Daily Mirror*.

19

Toto,

I went to Cottesloe looking for the places where Dad lived and worked. Unfortunately the Pavilion that housed the Seacrest Restaurant overlooking the beach was bulldozed. Now it's a surfclub-cum-snacketeria.

Mostly I remember him in those kitchens by the sea. There was the Colombo when I was really small, then later the Seacrest. At night, signs banging in the Fremantle southerlies, cyclists would wobble into sight by the neon and fishy hubbub of the pier, following the flickering of their own will-o-the-wisp light.

Inside, dapper in his heavy cotton coat and check trousers, Chef Alexander putting on his long waist apron and jaunty neckerchiefs. Ever the *manga.*

The climate in the kitchen was tropical in contrast with the air-conditioned cool of the restaurant itself overlooking a tangerine sunset on the Indian Ocean. Waiters, debonair in Eton jackets, would swing in carrying ice-tongs for the magnum coolers. Two worlds, Toto, separated by a swing door with a porthole window, two different kinds of theatre; theirs a pleasurable paradiso with its gleaming temptations of wall-mounted spirit-measures and blinding white linen; ours a kind of Hell of black iron frying pans and griddle scrapers.

In the deepest circle of Hell is butchery—the carving tables with cleavers and swivel hooks, fin shears and cruel-looking fillet knives.

At the heart of this armoury of hewing and hacking and spilling of blood was a friendly kitchen hand—an ex-wrestler, a Greek—they called the Professor. Bald as a billiard ball under his forage cap, and straight as a ramrod, he smiled as though he had a knife in his teeth.

I would move around the kitchen chatting. But when things heated up around 8 p.m. or 9, I would be sequestered to the temperate zone near the pantry and be given tasks like butter curling. There the waitresses would come looking for sundae cups and soda spoons and cocktail shakers. Away from the prong-forks and boning knives, my context—in an area pastellised by flour—became the gentler modelling tools made of wood. The vocabulary of pastry represents the *soigné* side of cooking, with a coquetry all its own: tartlets, puffs, petit-fours, vol-au-vents, lady's fingers. There are little deep savarins of crème caramel, fluted boats, flowery brioches, pomponettes.

There were little metal cutters too—crinkled and oval, stars and half-moons, hexagons and teardrops. There were animals and number moulds and alphabets. This association of food preparation and language extended to the piping tubes— a sort of pen for writing on cakes. My father—your grandfather, Totty—garnished desserts with star-ribbons and left-hand roses. A florid calligraphy. His own signature like a serpent doubling up to escape. Or palm trees in westerlies. Or grasshoppers singing in Greek.

Food and language, Toto, get mixed on menus throughout the world. A kind of kitchen language of mashed quotatoes: Mixed Gorilla, Smashed Homelletes, Fried Brian, Onion's Liver and Pork Throat. My father too minced his words, chopping and blending polyglot idioms into a mishmash of appetising jargon. At the Cafe Parisien, situated in Hay Street in the Cremorne Arcade next to Bon Marche, way back in 1932 his menu listed: *'fillet mignon à la sauce meiveillause,* cutlets *de veau pannes,* rolled cabbage *à la Parisienne,* spaghetti *à l'Italiana,* brains *à la sauce piquante* and special fish *au four à la Colbert'.* I kid you not. Pardon his French—but feel free to correct it my little *petit pois.*

The Ritz-Escoffier stranglehold on cuisine was the cause of this *franglais,* and the impregnable superiority of the French. Haute Cuisine was the Modernist canon. But in Perth in the early 1930s it must have appeared hoity-toity and surreal.

Food is a nation's petri-dish. Today's culture represents a kaleidoscope of materials and results. Now, Toto, we are postmodern. Now we can get Thai pizza, crab felafel salad, red pepper tahini. Or hoisin-sauced beef in a stiff moo shu pancake or wholemeal linguini with anchovy and pine-nuts.

I'm telling you this, Toto, because the details get forgotten.

Australia has become a whole lot of cultures sitting on top of each other smelling each other's restaurant exhaust fans. But it wasn't long ago that everything was obstinately vernacular: Hot Dog, Meat Pies and Mash. As Australia was part of the Commonwealth (really just a collection of cricket grounds), what persisted right up to the early 1970s was the imperialism of *à l'anglais*—a derogatory term, in Simon Loftus' words, for all things boiled for too long or fried after being dipped in egg and breadcrumbs. Today my father's cuisine (effortful cooking, with hearty but nuanced results) once thought grotesque is deigned perfectly yesable by most of my friends, and yours—sherried baby squid, fried Greek cheese, roasted peppers, okra.

Dad's polyglot background was genuine—he spoke five languages. He even knew *jeux d'esprit* that relied for their wit on a combination of Greek and French: *Depuis che je l'atrev, zestanov la flogue d'estimat, che mi pirpolis che mi gargalev, jusqu' à ton pat...*

By day Dad prepared and catered. The kitchen had the tang of soaking potato peels and sacks of empty oyster shells. Out of tinny speakers would come the mesmerizing race-calls from Randwick—a whiny chant, urgent, the stirring of a hardscrabble rhythm track that was part horse footfall, part something else something slower, aboriginal. The effect is like a trawler dragging nets against the tide of the ocker, cockneyfied wail, as though coming up from out of the ground sounding like: *I bin follerim I bin follerim I bin follerim I bin tracka I bin tracka I bin tracka, him bin raceaway...*

Inhaling cigarettes like long painkillers, he would wait for the results, and if his horse won—a three-legged horse with a nice name that came to him in a dream—he would sing in his smoky tenor, those half-Greek half-Arabic songs of his Cairo youth. *Ach ya ha bibi, ach ya leilleyli ah / Ta diosou hili stassoune meli, ah-ah...* The arms would go out, the fingers click and the funkified belly dance would include me, filling the space in a sea of Smyrnaic feeling. *Waha dit nen, waha dit nen, Anawa yak ya ha bibi layen ...* mixing yearning and cele-bration, dredging up a benign hashish house melancholy, with wild and unexpected atonalities spinning off like warped electrons.

By the 1970s he was tired of running restaurants. He tried working for others. One job he got, to be near me in Sydney—after my mother remarried, and we moved with my step-father to Bondi—was at the Travel Lodge, Rushcutters Bay. Here the semiology of food was based on portion control. He had to measure out slices of cheese. He didn't last long. He retired soon after.

Portion control, the microwave, the McDonald's 'cover version' of food was all *skata*—shit—to him. My father would not have survived this effort to turn the world into a giant no smoking zone. (I recall him taking out tobacco—a blend of Turkish and Virginia—and laying it on a handkerchief, taking a swig of cognac and gently spraying it. I remember him putting rosewater in his nargileh).

Toto—my little mischief, my UFO, my not-too-French french bean—what's in store for you? The seed companies are being taken over by the petro-chemical industries. Today they're altering the genes of fruit. They pick them green and gas them for Safeways: your mother comes back with impregnable peaches, heartless pears, permanent tomatoes. They may reach maturity but never ripen—this mutation has appeared naturally in humans for generations.

George thought of what not to write next, but made a note to himself. He was thinking of how this mutation in fruit connected with the 2-D hamburgers Toto was getting an appetite for—their cottony bread, the floury elastic paste they made in the mouth, mixed with pickle; and then with an irrational leap to what George thought of as Shake's unearned 'attitude'. George could see it too in the glossy images from *TeenGirl* magazine that covered Totty's walls. In the beautiful men conveying a mastery that never sweats; in the languid girls of the catwalks, like consumptive waifs. But he wrote nothing, fearing to be misconstrued.

> Your grandfather knew what 'ripeness' was: the sense that we belong in the world, and everything to its season. Kyriakos lived through his changes, and adapted the Greek cultural codes of *glendi* (good times), *kouvendes* (conversation) and *kali parea* (precursor of the rave) to Cottesloe. And it percolates, like the bubbling nargileh, from this thing the Greeks call *keyfi*—a mellow mood or Orientalised ambience you come across in the coffee houses where *kif* is smoked. People gather or drift in silence or talk among themselves in such a way that time and the world outside is entirely forgotten. Time may flow or lie around in pools.
>
> Here in Perth I saw him coming to me through a crowd full of sidewalk strollers in Hay Street, holding a parcel, a gardenia in his lapel. He had that East Med sallowness, unlike Greek pallor. A light-skinned negro with looks halfway between Jose Ferrer and Duke Ellington. Heavy build, appearance of

lackadaisical piracy. Listening to music, his head would tip back and he'd be cut free. He had the voice of a tenor, and when he smiled telling one of his stories, the corners of his mouth seemed to turn up and down at the same time, trying to find words for the countless schemes he had in mind.

George tore off another page and wrote:

Doctor: In my generation we knocked ourselves out to be like everyone else in Australia. Blonde people surrounded by blonde furniture. We tried to assimilate even though we knew there was something comical in all this. There was little public sanction to let you be yourself in the pre-1960s with its massively overcodified notions of national identity. Then we submitted democratically to the multicultural ideal. Out of affection and goodwill I've made gestures of normalcy: husband, citizen, father, householder. But instead of a society, it was a ruined artist's god to whom I prayed, over my shoulder.

Re: Writing Cure. It might be working. Writing is nature's consolation prize for dying. Choosing to be a writer, I realise now, is like my father's gambling and his forwarding addresses: for words are half-way houses to lost objects; they promise residence elsewhere. Words are IOUs, promissory notes, the detailed but utterly plausible IOUs of a gambler whose word has nonetheless proven unreliable. No wonder I've found it so hard to make a final downpayment on Love. But here I go psychoanalysing myself. You'll be out of a job.

20 After strawberries soaked in lemon juice and brown sugar, Alys readjusted her position within the scenario created by Zoë. She looked like Jean Seberg's St Joan. Her neck ached, her back ached, her flesh felt stranded, naked under the flash umbrella and the blind iris of the silver bromide. She was beginning to feel imprisoned by the high walls of Zoë's imagination, this dream she was constructing, this temple inside her head. Zoë told her several times to stop moving, as she kept changing the details in the background. Alys held her stare on the edge of the kilim's fusky fringe.

Zoë asked, 'Did George ever tell you how we were mugged in Fez? A hash deal that went wrong. Three guys had followed us from Ketama, cornering us finally at the wrong end of the medina. Two grabbed George and the one with the cadaverous face ran after me as I took off screaming. Out of the corner of my eye I saw George go down fighting. The rest was a blur of Coke ads in Arabic. I was leaping craters in the street and the guy behind was hitching up his djellaba. That slowed him down, by which time people gathered and he pulled back, but not before he cut me under the ear. Here. I've still got the scar. I've never been so scared. Soon after, nose bloodied, George arrived. He was laughing, I was shaking. They'd taken our money, passports, the hash, everything.

Later, in Malaga, in a tattoo shop smelling of jasmine and leaky sewers, we got our snakes.'

Alys knew. How could she not know. Both had snakes eating their tails high on the shoulder. It was a connection.

Alys had caressed and kissed both, dizzy with the roundabout of deflected desires. Every person has six sides like a die.

Her neck hurt. Zoë's eyes and the arc lamps devoured her. She thought about Toto coming home from school soon. She felt anxious. She felt as if imprisoned inside Zoë's fantasy of reprisal. It had felt at first like an occasion to jump out of herself, to let her freely roaming subjectivity play act the victim, in shadow material. Now these stories about George. Until this moment she had kept unconnected somehow. Up to now she had one itinerary, to explore this flooding of female pleasures; to give in to the electric charm of an affair with another partner. But she was at present charmed into paralysis like a cobra in Djemma el Fna.

Desire was never transparent. It was always displaced and now she felt caught up in this circuit of misdirection. What seemed liberatory now felt like the inner mirrorings of a dandy's wardrobe. Didn't she prefer herself reflected in Zoë's body to Zoë herself? Didn't she prefer her image of Zoë to Zoë achieved? She felt a shadow-person, a peeled snail that wanted her shell back.

'In Barcelona', Zoë continued, her voice no longer as clear, now hardening, now quivering, 'there was the telegram waiting at the American Express regarding Rory's death. Accident? Suicide? It was a thunderbolt. It hit between the eyes like a low door. I realised my life had two eras. A time which pre-dates that telegram and the time which followed. We were transformed. For the better? I'm not sure. From being in love to being in limbo. I was stone. George's body crawled inside his

105

mind and stayed there. Our bold forward strides across conti-
nents felt like the pawing of a hamster wheel. It wasn't long
before our sex life went kind of matte, you know. Like those
aching moments when you recognise foreplay has gone on for
too long.'

Alys held her stare at the edge of the rug, fiddling with
the dirty fringe.

On TV the jets shrieked, and so did the canned laughter. The trailers for the new sit-com were interspersed with shots of oil rigs ablaze in the Persian Gulf. The new show would keep us in stitches. The world is already in stitches. Wait till they take them out.

George penned a quick question on another postcard to the Doctor:

Is a sense of humour a sign of health in a videoleptic, or is a sense of humour the cruellest and most dangerous part of the illness? P.S. Should I put all my money in laughing stocks?

Then he rang Alys and told her that he had talked to his grandfather, that Yiorgos had stood in the dining room at City Beach with his back to the window. And he's been dead for forty years.

'What was he wearing?' asked Alys.

'A faded blue fisherman's cap, and he was holding a coil of light nylon line.'

'Doesn't anything happen to anyone else?', screamed Alys. 'It all happens to you.'

'What?'

'I'm sorry George. I'm not buying your excuse that historical drag justifies your behaviour.'

'He's had an era-change operation', quipped Zoë in the background. 'Give me a dedicated female impersonator any-time.'

George half-listened, looking across the backyard at three men carrying a mist around them with the blue-green colours of a mirror. George recognised Manolis hobbling around on a broken leg, after he had been kicked by a pack-horse in Syria. Kyriakos was having his head shaved while smoking a nargileh under the aqueous blue light trapped in the plastic covered awnings of the neighbours' shed. The other one was Yiorgos. But while he was over the back fence he was in the room as well, where George was talking to Alys on the phone. If on the principle of *to fade out* you could say *to fade in*, that's how Yiorgos entered the room. Like a creep of cool air under the door. He could just see the trousers with sand in the cuffs.

'Stop raking up the past. It just brings it all up. Old ghosts, shit, mould, broken bottle, snails—the whole bloody paella. Leave it alone.'

'You encouraged me to. You said take a vacation. You said do something by doing nothing. You don't understand what it's like. Everything is in double exposure. I'm booking a flight to Cairo. Then Athens. Then Kastellorizo. I'll see you in fourteen days. I've got to exorcise these demons.'

'Oh why don't you throw yourself off an ouzo bottle. You're out of your socket. What about Bones? I'm sick of this back and forth. Sick of it.'

'Give me time, Alys.'

'Give *me* time.'

There was a long silence.

'I'll put him in the cattery. Your folks are due back soon anyway. Twelve steps away from landing on this doorstep. I'll make them a meatloaf. Leave it in the fridge. With rum in it.'

Alys slammed the phone down. When would the ghosts of his ancestors recede? It was embarrassing for herself and her friends, all of whom had clearly disowned their parents long ago. Who believes in ghosts? People whose body temperature changes a shade either way from 37 degrees centigrade? What could ghosts be? The rise of heat off the tarmac if you were a sceptic. What's a soul? A kind of ultrahigh frequency software? Aretha Franklin doing her vibrato and those Motown shouts?

Zoë said his grandparents were still alive, because it was something George never gave them credit for when they *were* alive. Zoë quoted Larkin, bachelor, to Alys:

They fuck you up, your Mum and Dad
Man hands on misery to man
It deepens like a coastal shelf
Get out as early as you can
And don't have any kids yourself.

At the other end of the line George felt depressed again at City Beach. He sensed he could be screwing his relationships up. He sensed Zoë hovering in the background. Sometimes one person was not enough, and yet deep inside he always wanted one person to be enough.

George looked around the room. He put away his writing into the manila folder. He tore up the letter from the head of the sub-titling department. It had a threatening tone. He guessed his poor colleagues were going to hell in an in-basket tray. He looked enviously at the photo of Violetta and Kyriakos in Port Said in the years before he was born. Mother at the table, a Durrellian beauty with a knockout smile, her hair long and lustrous. My father wearing a tarboush, the red fez that is the mark of the Egyptian gentry, seated across from her, looking at the camera somewhat vainly. The cousins are dressed impeccably even on a hot summer's day. George wanted to crawl into the frame. He had come to believe that all that was good about his family took place in these years before he was born, and ended shortly afterwards.

Alone or married? That was the question. Mr and Mrs Mouse at a lifelong Tupperware party? Or the bitter bite of bachelors? Life was a series of intractable vs. Men vs Women. The toilet seat up vs the toilet seat down. Rapture vs capture. Passion vs domesticity. Freedom vs enslavement. Compatibility vs good sex. Single vs sewn up. Let's grow roses on Sunday vs Let's heave our luggage over the globe.

He thought about his life before Alys, before Zoë. He liked it. Not the loneliness. Not at 4 a.m. in the morning. But because it felt *in the world*. Alys was the first person he felt he could live with and still be in the world—an addition to his life, not an abdication of it. More months of traipsing back and forth between apartments seemed senseless. Her kitchen chairs went with his. And a friend of Alys who had just stopped living with Alys said she'd finish her lease, but Alys could keep the key, maintain visiting rights and have the flat back if it came to that. Both George and Alys were islomanes: they loved islands. They were married on Rottnest Island. But it wasn't long after all the initial socialising in twosies (Mr and Mrs Possum visiting Mr and Mrs Rabbit) before they had plunged into the pit of urban middle class nuclear familydom; it wasn't long before the love affair dissolved into a Mum-and-Dad sandmover's combine, eroding all other human relationships and leaving them stranded on Mortgage Island.

And of course wives know husbands in a hardboiled way. On the other hand the regime of the solitary life? Dinner is fillet of sole in front of a program on the vascular system. Sounds OK? Sounds horrible. Singles become totally self-absorbed, can't play off self from other. Can couples?

George Alexander couldn't cope either way. Then there was Toto and Alys and all the real detail and substance of their lives in Bondi. That electric current running between the three of them.

At the enormous desk there was also Toto's drawings she had sent her grandparents when she was five. George remembered how she covered one crayon with a blanket of paper and put it to beddie byes. 'The pencil's dreaming', she said. George missed her, George missed them both. You survive presumably, he thought, but there is less of you.

'In every person's life how much is indescribable, or if described unbelievable, or if believed, brutalised.' Christopher Morley, copyright, 1949.

The Arabic voice from the old 78 record is dragging out the song, passionate, irrational, driven. And the time-milking ululations of the Middle East gather like a tide. The wailing mixes with muffled sounds from the streets of East Perth and the sun warming my arms and Dad silhouetted in the kitchen, and Toto resting one hand lightly in mine and with her other holding her bottle to her mouth, letting the bubbles hiss through the teat opening, like some nursery nargileh, and everything seemingly connected. Mother's voice joining Fairuz and the light bouncing off the lino highlighting Alys' eyes of candlelit amber, and Toto's touch, like in a picture, caught forever, in the heart always, outside of time, patiently waiting for dinner. Waiting with neither resolve nor resignation, just adrift in that comfy now. And behind it all a kind of triumph made up of loss, a certainty that the worst would always be behind us, and love wiring us all together in an oddly festive sorrow.

22

That night the darkness came down, as full as the moon before the night has nibbled it. Yiorgos wore a fez and the moonlight was on it. I could see his outline. He came so quietly I didn't know he was there.

'So you're *George Alexander.*' He spat the name with contempt. 'Have you murdered Yiorgos yet?'

'Have a gin.'

'A djinn?'

I poured the gin. Handed it to him. But he was gone. I had a shooting pain in my left side.

I saw him cross the heath to the beach. I followed. The sky broke, peppermint trees began to complain, the sea was a mild fever of grey and white, of water, and gulls and rolling shells. Up ahead islands of clouds, and light leaving first the limestone cliffs, then the sea, then the sky.

Along the sand, with the tide going out, he picked up a channelled whelk, its shape blurred with moss; then a double sunrise like the wings of the butterfly translucent white. Just as he did as a child. Now there was the stray pineapple top, and the battery caps, and the tampon dispensers as well.

Yiorgos walked with swaying steps. He wore overalls like a mechanic's, with a name stitched on the back. But every time I thought I was able to read it the folds got in the way. The first three letters looked like MOR. And then AL. And there was a T in there somewhere. But what bothered me was that he was carrying a parcel that looked like the mysterious jiffybag in my safe.

'Hey, that's mine', I croaked. But he disappeared into a break in the dunes and began to climb the narrow path.

Looking back, I saw only one set of footsteps, my own. I saw the shapes they made. The walk guided by the random shells had all the signs—looking back—of determination. Chance had become destiny. Form was in the footsteps looking back.

There was a girl, about Toto's age, on her own. The wind blew her skirt against her legs, her jacket back from her young breasts. The wind tattered the clouds, now strands of ochre scud.

It was dark by the time he got to the road. He took out a cigarette, and as he struck the match, he sensed something else—an impressive display of fireworks exploding behind his eyeballs. The last thing he remembered, in slow motion, was his foot parting from one shoe—stop—try and reinsert the foot, prise it up with humped toes. Blackout. He didn't feel the blow, just saw the stabbing crimson lights riding on a wave of nausea before he fell into a deep blackness.

I buried him in a sandpile with a council shovel. The sand was as heavy as an historical novel. Everything was crackling with electricity too, as if one had been shuffling over a synthetic carpet. After digging for an hour, there was Yiorgos still on the mound.

'You might have spared me the labour.'

'I spare you nothing.'

The wind caught the ash of his cigarette and blew it on the sand. I put away the shovel and fell on the bed.

114

That same night in Sydney, Alys donned her helmet, left Glebe, and headed for Toto and Bondi. It was a decision of great simplicity. Zoë waved goodbye with one hand, a film broadsheet in the other. The phonecall on top of everything else that afternoon put a deadly layer of starch over the day.

After the photo-shoot the mood became self-conscious with Zoë recharging the ever-empty vessels of small-talk with a kind of anxious fun. Then she said restlessness would find no answer in flight—and Alys thought she was talking about *her*, not George.

How quickly jubilation leads to fear. Nirvana *à deux* could be fractured by a telephone ringing. A lover becomes 'a situation'. Zoë remained a space, a question. Like her photographs Zoë offered a pure emulsion on which she could expose startling negatives.

Alys had to re-establish her boundaries. A moment ago she was a heat-seeking organism, four legs, four arms, two faces. Then she was opaque skin before the camera. Now she had to pull the drawstring of her flesh together, the parts that had fallen away from her soul—whatever that was—and hold on to Toto. That's all she knew.

Through the visor of the full-face helmet, the edge of the road and the trees on the other side blurred as her 1000 cc Ducati rode the ripples in the bitumen. There was a slight sideways twist as the shaft drive torqued the bike over fractionally on full throttle in second and a faint graunch as the right hand pipes touched the tarmac. The bike was howling. A flash pinpointed a car coming into a tight right hander from the opposite direction and Alys moved her knee in close to the bike allowing it to drift away from the white line marking the road's centre. For a moment her senses failed to register things correctly and the bike took time and motion from her, and then mercifully created its own level and Alys, crying now, went with it.

That night Alys dreamt they were in a huge hotel in North Africa. She was following Zoë down circuitous corridors. When she went ahead, sudden bursts of noisy tourists came between them. When she caught up to Zoë, Zoë pulled her to her, held her. But by now Zoë was George, saying: 'Don't worry. It will be lovely.'

23 That same night George dreamt of Alys, pregnant. It's after his father died. Fearing a fire, he is giving her a copy of his father's book to put in the safe. He would keep the other upstairs in the office. Somehow he has taken the copy downstairs to the living room, where Alys is keeping the first copy until she can get it to the safe. This is foolish because now if there was a fire both copies would be lost. In one further image, Alys puts a copy in a secret cabinet in the stove. If the manuscript is put in the stove, it is brought in relation to fire—the last place you'd look if there was a fire. And yet even if the stove should burn up, the manuscript would be saved being completely enclosed in metal.

The next morning the phone rang. I couldn't answer it. I couldn't talk. The instrument itself might noose me with its constricting tensile twists. It rang again. I picked it up. It was Doctor Nemerov.

I told him about the dream. He said that putting the book in the safe was an attempt to defeat death. The act represented vanity, ego, false security. He said the copy was the child.

'The child?', I wondered. 'The one in the womb?'

'The living room is where you live with Alys and Toto. Your work is keeping them out. The stove is the bun in the oven. Stove's burn hot with passion, but are safe. The *living* room is the challenge you face: bringing to life both your dead father and your unborn child. Accept…'

Something cut us off. How did he know about the unborn child? Did everybody know? Whose unborn child?

The rest of the day George Alexander packs up. Throws his clothes into the Moroccan barrel bag. Takes cat to the cattery. Rings Belacqua Toth to tell him he's leaving. It's OK. Toth says Bluey is heading to the airport to pick up a consignment. Bluey could give you a lift.

Nothing narrows a person more than travel, thought George. Start out with grand plans and soon you're bogged down with minutiae: passports, tickets, inoculations, schedules. Why not go home to Bondi with all the familiar things: my friends, my phone, my stuff? Hadn't he always believed that we were all in the middle of a journey, anyhow? Aren't our lives the journey? Why waste time with other itineraries?

Next day Bluey arrived in a primer-grey Valiant, wearing a frilled cowboy shirt, dark glasses and an 'Australia' windcheater. After driving off at breakneck speed, Bluey put the car on cruise control once they'd hit the Sterling Highway and relaxed into the pneumatic rhythm of the tarmac. The angry chortle of Bluey's V8 engines, and the mellow Country and Western, blended like booze and Valium. Somehow it helped George regain some of his calm. Bluey grew up out west of Katanning— where George as a one-year-old had spent some time. George told Bluey he had had an Aboriginal lady friend of his parents babysitting him. This wasn't allowed, this fraternising with the blacks. But Kyriakos and Violetta liked Auntie Flo. One day Auntie Flo took off with him out to show her mob the baby. A white baby against the bright-red dune sand of the gum and acacia scrublands around Pingrup way. Country of dreams. 'Your country one little bit cranky', Florence would say to Violetta.

'You could get an eye infection doing that', said Bluey, turning the volume up on the dashboard twang. Out there was the debil-debil, that fella sit alonga scrub, go alonga sky, then bang crash goodbye, Pinish, no come back. Bluey had been urbanised overnight. He had a thirst for it. But Bluey's radar was tuned to a landscape that was all vanishing points, while the rest of his senses hummed with the constant, dusty, meaningless forward motion along the highways of Western Australia.

'What's this then?', asked Bluey, pointing to the luggage on George's lap, ' "Operation Run For it?" '

'I've been a dickhead' said George.

'Ya not gettin an argument from me on that one, mate', said Bluey.

They exchanged a look.

George showed Bluey pictures of Alys and Toto, while thinking about the inevitable: trust Zoë to grab any loose livewires of desire and hold on. Toto's sad oval face like a planet. Alys in a pumpkin coloured shirt, with a bored-heiress-at-Cannes circa-1972 look.

'But you know sex is not a battlefield that women always lose.'

'No, no, fair enough', said Bluey. Communication with Bluey would never be speech. Sport, or shared work perhaps— setting the rusty fox-trap, hanging rabbit-skins on stretchers; or just the silent self-containment expected of a people who spent years not seeing anybody. *Cris de coeur* weren't in the vernacular, and anybody having a nervous breakdown was 'just acting sorta funny'. Bluey's territory was all straight edge and pre-psychological.

They listened to the words of the next record on the radio. Dusty Springfield. Her name alone conjured a kind of parched yearning, a snookered hope. *You know in the end, when it's time to descend, there's no easy way down...*

Meanwhile, back at the home at City beach, while George Alexander was heading for Perth International Airport, Alys was leaving a long message on the answer-phone for him.

'1,2,3,4 testing', she began. 'You're all I ever wanted in a man. You're brave, sweet, smart ... in some ways you're a much better person than I am. I'm tired ... I'm just too tired to live with you anymore. Even measured against your personal losses ... you're too complicated, you demand too much of me, of people ... And you've become wall-eyed, always looking a bit to the left or right of where I'm actually standing. Or think I'm standing. Zoë ... she opened wide for me. I opened wide for her. Now my heart has expanded to include another ... Hello, George? Are you there? Listen. A lawyer rang. From the notary's office. There's a release date on your father's property by the end of the month. Bye. I love you.'

24 Wherever you go, there you are. George sat in the airport lounge—coffee shop? cafenion? cantina?—what was it? George sat there not moving a muscle. Why was he here? Why was he always, more or less, here? He could go wherever he wanted, go where he liked, but he knew he'd always find himself, with slight variation, in the same place, at the same point. Always somewhere. Always *nel mezzo del cammin,* Dante's dark forest.

Overhead the Translux News Jet signboards were pixel-lating destinations. The telex-programmed machines picked out green fluorescent letters from the dot-configurations on the regularly rotated rectangular flaps. He looked up at the names on the screen: *Kastellorizo, Cairo, Cottesloe, Karrakatta.* Anagrams of each other, they were generating a secret narrative out of control: *Castel Rosso. Red Castle. Cairo. Kao. Chaos. Cot. Cottesloe.*

The mind was a labyrinth. 'In the middle of the path of my life I found myself in a dark forest, for the straight path had been lost.' The loss of the straight path was not the problem. The problem was that straight paths had proliferated. Life had become all *mezzo,* all middle and all muddle. But there was some consolation: it was impossible to take an aimless itinerary. For example: take a random walk blindfolded away from a lamp post. Change direction according to whim. Move in a wholly irregular fashion. The law of disorder predicts you will keep returning to the lamp post. The twenty-six-year-old Einstein made a reputation in physics on it.

121

In the souvenir shop George picked up a vinyl hairbrush in the shape of a boomerang. When you turned the winding key it played "Waltzing Matilda". 'I don't mind living like this,' thought George. 'I can't bear living like this.'

Every airport is the same. Around him people stammered in one another's tongues, exchanged each other's luxury goods, changed each other's money and admired each other's glamour. In the transit lounge the whole globe appears in complex seductive relationships to itself, the erotic differences at play always merging into the same old scene where really only one language is spoken: Wieviel kostet? C'est combien? How much? Quanto?

George booked his flight at the registration desk. How singularly pointless, thought George, are our papers of identification. Who are you by the way? When? Often? Significantly so? Soon the seemingly motionless speed of the 747 would make a twisted nonsense of time and space too; soon Cairo would seem closer than Kalgoorlie; soon the blazing lozenges of light in the cabin at 60,000 feet would mean noon or midnight, and feel like both.

Before long they had hit the cloudline and the cabin rocked from side to side. The old Greek next to George, who wanted him to set up his duty-free Walkman, was already asleep. The tape was still rolling. Out the window between the cottony clouds the ground was like stretched animal hide, and George could just make out bulldozers priming the red clay, buckling the thin crust of asphalt like pork crackling, scarring the earth, building theme-parks. Perth burning behind us in the cross-lighting, like one of Lot's cities.

Before long the fuselage was enclosed in the black unbreathable nowhereness of flight. Inside, the window gave back reflections—noses, brows, glasses, creamy shirt fronts—human presences picked out by the track-lights against a geologic blackness. My hair looked like a temporary wig, my likeness reflected an absence.

By the time the stewardess arrived with the clinking drinks caddy, my lap-strap wearing companion had regained consciousness.

'*Pios ise?*', he asks with an anis smell on his breath. For a Greek of this generation 'who are you?' means 'which clan do you belong to?'. Even third-generational Kastellorizians know the answer—the Dondas clan. Alexandroglou was your real name, but Dondas was your *paratsoukli*, or nick-name.

'*Me xeris?* Don't you know me? I'm Dondas. I've aged. I was a sea-captain then. *Then me xeris?*'

He asks this of everyone passing down the aisle of the plane. And he knows everyone, or so he claims. He's like a clairvoyant feeding names: Manolis? Kyriakos? Farouk? Port Said? Panama?

'*Piasse tho!*', or 'Press the flesh', he says offering his hand. Like blacks in New York 'giving skin'. Offering his freckly hand with its big gold ring. Passing on some mantle of patriarchal order, some secret tribal honour, like the long capitals of my name.

Shall I tell him I'm embroiled in a search for my past, which I am trying to put in a narrative? I am like proliferating crab-grass; he, one of the thick branches of the family tree.

What's more the intricate strands of autobiography are endless and would bore him. The language I use, take refuge in, makes me socially weightless everywhere I go. That's because I'm caught between languages, each language—Greek, Italian, English, street, academic—each vetoes the other. I have no flag, no Union Jack, no tarboush, no Akubra to call my own. I change at each site of my incarnation. I'm here to make the Greeks feel more Greek, the Australians more Australian, the Brits more British, but what am I?

I tell him I'm a teacher, *daskalos*. That seemed grounded enough. For the rest of the trip I am *daskale. Pes mou daskale:* tell me teacher… His flesh is the colour of yellowing piano keys, old texts. His anis and peanutty smell is masked by residual eau-de-cologne and gritty talcums.

'What are you listening to?' I ask.

'*Nissiotika.*'

There was a tinny sound coming from his headphones. I could make out the singer dragging out the song, with time-cheating melisma, with hyberbolic wailing—frantic, jittery, wired-up, over the top—lasting ninety minutes. Then at last there was a different silence in the cabin, a silence that had been advanced upon and won, not retreated into.

Somewhere over the Somali Basin a phone started to ring. I ignored it. I hadn't left a number where I could be reached, but the ringing got louder. The stewardess, carrying the phone on a little zinc tray, came down the aisle towards me. I sat up and tried to look nonchalant.

'It's for you', she said.

I leaned out of the bed and groggily picked up the phone. But the ringing wouldn't stop.

'Are we there yet?'

My travel alarm clock had woken me up. Cairo interruptus.

As the plane proceeded with its descent, Yiorgos said, '*Efagame to vothi, tora mono i oura.*' We've eaten the ox, now only the tail remains.

We disembarked the plane and walked across the tarmac. The air you could cut into cubes and ship to Tasmania. On entering the terminal I headed for the immigration desk and presented my passport. In the baggage area Arabs in uniforms hung all over me to take my luggage. I resisted, retrieved my bag and chose a porter who took it through custom checks. Yiorgos told me under no circumstance to go all the way to the street with bags.

Somehow, while I was scanning the reception area for hotel information, a persistent taxi driver at my elbow had put the bag where it was not supposed to be—out on the street.

By the time I reached it, my bag was being fought over by about half a dozen youths at each other in Arabic. I had only Australian currency and my smallest bills were two tens. The porter put his hand out for one, and then disappeared.

I climbed into the battered black and white Peugeot while three or four of the more aggressive guys wrestled my bag into the trunk. I offered one my last tenner, telling him to split it with the others. As the taxi pulled into traffic, the youth who claimed he was 'in charge' hung in the window demanding something for himself and letting me know, in Arabic, what a cheap Anglo bastard he thought I was.

Then I noticed the driver was not the man I had negotiated the fare with, but he knew the way to Lofti Hassouna Street and spoke a serviceable English.

'First time in Al-Qahira?'

'Not really.' I stared at the city camouflaged by sand to look like the desert. The largest city of Africa, its chief commercial entrepot and the centre of Arab culture and music. Place of my conception and the necropolitan capital of the world. Moslems, Copts, Jews, Greeks, Italians, Maltese, Cypriots, Indians. Over the last few centuries the foreigners were the stock speculators and vice peddlers. Protected by Capitulations, they took jobs in local consular offices, were interpreters, or attachés for British or US diplomatic missions. They set up canals, paved streets, piped water, set up gas lights, cotton gins, sugar refineries, telegraph lines. While the fellaheen had the highest infant mortality rate in the world.

A city, too, of indefatigable street hustlers. From the taxi in hot twilight I see a man with a tambourine lead a slim-waisted, crimsoned-arsed baboon from a choker around his full mane. A woman assisted by her four-year-old daughter puts a can of benzene to her mouth, applies a torch, and breathes a ferocious blast of flame. Is it Alys with Toto? No. Not in this city of Citroëns and donkeys. I see a boy crouch, staring blankly, taking a shit. Impressions in paint, in mud, of children's hands against the walls of squalid streets. The Khamseen, the desert wind, blows sand through keyholes in the doors shut against it. The *sukkas*, or water-carriers, sprinkle water from their goatskins to lay the dust.

The Bab El-Azab gateway, meanwhile, is lined with poles on which are stuck the heads of 450 British soldiers.

The cabbie drops me off at Dokki, at the steps of the Faros Hotel. He has some kind of deal going. No, *no son et lumière* at the Pyramids. I was having enough *son et lumière* all on my own and it didn't cost me any piastres.

'Port Said. You take me there?'

'Insh'allah. God Willing.' If I want to visit Port Said he would take me he says, leaving his number. 'Good morning', he says, though it's night now.

25

The room was in some retarded twentieth century style. It smelled of freshly glued vinyl tiles and damp sheetrock. The AC didn't work, the music system didn't work, but there was a fantastic old bakelite phone out of a 1940s film noir.

The room was a double with two single beds. Lying on one bed, made you feel you were disoccupying the other. Coming back to the room, after a visit to the registration desk, made me feel the presence of an implied absence, or the other way around, the absence of an implied presence. Yiorgos Alexandroglou? Had I signed in under that name?

The two armchairs were angled accusingly at each other, as in a war room. The mirror was an odd parallelogram. It might even have been upside down. In the low-wattage of the overhead light, it gave back an older man with a gut-heavy look and a hairline beating a retreat. I was 40 and he looked 60.

I headed for the restaurant downstairs. As I am doing so—against odds no gambler would take—Yiorgos is coming up. 'The way up and the way down are the same' he says. It's like finding a kangaroo killed in an elevator.

Jet-lag or more spiralling reality dislocation? A series of slip-ups, events ordered sight unseen. Reality can do flip-flops. Like the train at the station—the flying platform down the immobile tracks; the city flowing through the motionless cabin—which moves first?

As I take my place at the buffet, all lustres of polished copper, I see my double rise and move out of the shadows. As

I rise and look out the window (tribal Hyksos horse soldiers, Libyans, Cushites, Assyrians, North African Fatimids, Circassian slaves), I am at the same time sitting at the table eating my dinner at 12 Lofti Hassouna St, Dokki, Cairo, 1990.

I couldn't shake off Yiorgos. He was all over me like a cheap suit. I put aside my plate of fuul and ta'amiyya. Of all the family members to pick on, why me?

I couldn't shake off the double exposure. OK, I could be a pragmatist. Everything is coming through the mirror of George Alexander's imagination. That I knew. I was pushing forty and forty was pushing back.

Then I remember the doctor and the Writing Cure, and begin to regain some of my calm. I take out my notebook. Its leather cover I notice now has a few hairs growing back on the skin. As if time is running backwards an inch or two on its reel.

I'm freaked out; but Yiorgos isn't. It is Yiorgos. Casting a shadow in the room like a leaden-keeled boat on the bottom of the Mediterranean. I'm drowning, I can't breathe, while Yiorgos is humming something with Ya-ha-bibi in it. The dead roll on. I am conscious of him all the time now. He's as real as a bone in an X-ray. He is like my ghost-negative. I know Yiorgos isn't out there. He is making room for himself in my psyche. Slow and incessant Yiorgos floods George to overflowing.

I go back to the hotel room. I start a letter to Toto:

> The Greeks had been in Egypt since Alexander and the Ptolemies, dealing in silver, oil, wine. Now nothing but the name survives. There were Greek colonies in Smyrna, in the Panariot community of Constantinople, and some three thousand of them in Alexandria by the 1860s.

I put the biro down, light a match and bring it towards my mouth, but I'd forgotten to take the cigarette out of the packet. The left half of the brain controls this right hand, and logic, speech, sense of space. The right half of the brain controls the awkward left hand, suspicion, primal fear, our sense of time. With my frightened left side I confuse thumb and little finger, and burn myself.

'Salaam', he says, in a hieratic way. In place of speech, a clattering morse hammers out of his palate in Arabic. Indifferent-looking, his eyes seem made of the hardest material of the earth. A gaze, honestly, from way off the map.

It was Yiorgos sitting opposite me.

'Your writing deprives us of identity you know.' He says sadly, 'You offer an identity made only of letters ... once upon a time I kept you alive in my brain. You lived on a beautiful island called *In The Beginning*. I remembered the way to this Greek island. I could navigate the rocks, the currents, kept track of all the inhabitants. I knew the names of maybe 99 men, 116 women. Panayotta, Constantinius, Eleftheria, Loucas, Dhespina, Tyscos, Pandelis, Anastasia, Varvara, Dhionisia, Calliopi... Beyond the island lay Turkey, wilderness. Do the people there exist? Or did I invent them? On that penumbral margin, that Anatolian coast, there is confusion—sometimes sweet, sometimes terrifying—between memory and imagination.'

I was trying to adjust to my threshold of anxiety when he started off again, on another track: 'You! Your head is crammed with a million names', he says to me. 'The faces of public personalities, Terence Trent D'Arby or Eugene Terr' Blanche, Lee Majors or Lee Remick, the names of actors playing fictional characters, 'Seinfeld', people in Nike ads, aspiring sons and daughters of talk show hosts, people who sold the rights to their murder trial to the tabloids...'

I thought I'd try a Zen cream pie: 'So you're Yiorgos? Have you killed off George yet?'

He came back with one of his own: 'I am everyone you ever wanted to be. Including yourself.'

I felt guilty. I remembered City Beach. He still had sand in the cuffs of his trousers. There was a great gash on the back of his head. Then in a kind of chant:

'I'm Bones the cat. Have I been fed? I am the book. Have I been read? I'm the tissue of the brain, I'm the sudden little pain...'

Everything, as I say, was double exposure—seeing it this way with one skill of the brain, and that way with another. Hearing is in stereo too.

'I gotta get to the nearest payphone.'

'Leave it alone.'

'Then I'll turn on the radio.'

'No, no, no.'

'But what can I do?'

'Be you.'

Was I mistaking these phrases for the hubbub percolating up from the streets? There are chance misregistrations, like badly printed colour plates of the Levant. Footsteps echoing from the laneway.

What time was it? I had Australian time on my travel clock and Cairo time on my wrist watch.

The proportions of the hotel room were still unsettling, with a tendency to slip and drift. I was still looking at the scene across the mortal divide. Cigarette dangling from his lower lip, Kyriakos comes and goes. Sometimes he is there, then he flickers out. Manolis invades his silhouette like some putrefaction you find on cheese. Yiorgos is so bright I put on my Raybans, but realise it's only my eyes, filled with pain-photisms. He is wearing charms from ancient Egypt.

The place is hectic with the traffic of the dead. Now all three seem to walk through each other, like a group-mechanism. I went back to my tested narcotic: a double scotch. There was an air of suspended action in the room.

Behind galleries with metal lattice screens, wet-nurses take out their cafe-au-lait breasts to feed the European babies. A prophylactic against typhoid, a practice carried out since the time of the Pharaohs. Fatima is the *nourrice* for Kosta, while the older Alexandroglou boys play hide and seek up and down the rear stairs.

Under the frangipani and scarlet flame trees, men in white djellabas eat dried melon seeds and sip sherberts of lemonade. On pavement terraces at brass tables in basketwork chairs, my father drinks a now cloudy raki and hands out Partagas cigars he's just bought from the tobacconist in the Kasr el Nil. He's planning dancing with Violetta Lo Verso at the Semiramis, and gambling at the Paradiso. Failing either, picking up a Ghawazi girl to the northeast of the Ezbekieh Gardens. Failing that, well, there's always the brothels of Clot Bey, where girls tie scarves around their hips and do votive belly dances for their clients. Gyrations, ripplings, and a most erotic stillness. *Ya ha bibi, ya l'eillaili!*

Now Kyriakos brings his father-in-law, Alessandro Lo Verso—Violetta's father—the *Al Guihad* and the *Egyptian Gazette.* Looking dapper with the Blimpishness of Attlee's Britain: pipe, hair strictly *en brosse.* Flicks his flywhisk made of camel hair. The *ghiuffrah,* or supervisor of a transport company. Member of the trade guilds and masonic lodges. Both clubs: *La Casa D'Italia* and the Greek *Orfeo*. Half-Greek, half-Italian, Alessandro identified with the patrilineal line: the absent and bigamous Antonio, who had another wife and family in Buenos Aires. Profiling against Louis-Farouk furnishings: mahogany filing cabinets, marble tables, porcelain lamps, velvet curtains with bobble fringes. Listening to the fascist propaganda from Mussolini, broadcast from powerful radio transmitters set up in Bari. Drinking vodka and guava juice brought by a fezed Sudanese the colour of polished walnut. He was a desk man: twists his pencil to make lead appear. My father's side: decks, not desks; sailors, deck-hands, travellers. By the late 1930s the British—he worked for the NAAFI—start vetting personnel. With his Italian passport he seemed compromised. On 11 July 1940, in the early hours of the morning the District Security Officer took Aleko away, Violetta screaming. He was interned for five years in a hellish desert camp near Mansour. Then he had to start all over in Botany, Sydney, Australia. He took my mother in after the separation with Kyriakos in Perth. But his heart had by then gone dry with the need for system and order. 'Nothing', he would shout, 'is where I left it'. '*System! System!*' he used to bellow at me. He died gathering sawdust with a brushpan on the eve of my mother's second marriage.

Outside, taxis are full of Egyptians in Western-style clothes, and you hear angry shouts of *Istiklal el Tam*, 'Unconditional Independence'. A dead dog, rotting on a pavement, covered by flies. A boy practises writing on a tile, the Koran held open by two stones.

I decided to visit Port Said, and maybe Ismailia, the de Lesseps company town, and take a look at the Suez Canal. Built overnight, it might have been an Australian port city with a French accent, Newcastle crossed with Marseilles.

The next morning I called the cab driver, his name written in his own hand: 'Khada Ahzab'. The address: 'street, 27 of Korshid, Shopra'.

'Good night', he said, wishing me the wrong time of day and shaking my hands warmly.

For a while the drive was unremarkable: passing biblical villages, saw-toothed waterwheels drawing cups of water and splashing into straight channels disappearing to the cotton fields. When we reached Zagazig, the taxi swerved to the left across the oncoming line of traffic and screeched to a dusty halt on the side of the road.

'Gasoline', he grinned back at me. The Gulf War, he said, was making things difficult, as he ran off with three one-gallon plastic containers to a throng of Bedouins around a trestle table. He returned with them empty. He started the taxi and proceeded along the shoulder of the wrong side of the road, scattering pedestrians, attempting now and again to break across oncoming traffic.

Unable to force any opposing driver to allow him through, he wrenched the steering wheel to the right and floored it, causing a southbound Ford to go sideways in a full slide, missing the cab by the barest. My driver fishtailed back into the northbound lane, leaving a cacophony of squealing brakes and curses in his wake.

About a mile down the road, he pulled over and cut the engine. He grinned and gestured that he had to speak to a girl. He picked her up and she sat in the back smiling, eyes ringed with kohl. 'Girl', he grinned at me. Then he left us both in the car and went loping across the Cairo-Port Said road. Minutes later he returned. 'Gas', he grinned at me. With the grimy plastic containers he was off again. I watched as several men helped drain a gallon of gas from a 55-gallon drum on the side of the road, as he borrowed a tin funnel, as he danced back to the car through traffic, poured the container into his tank, dodged back to return the funnel. After a few more minutes talking with the girl, he drove off with a shrug and a chuckle, the girl singing along with Oum Kalsoum all the way.

We got to Port Said eventually. I hadn't experienced a drive like it since a motorbike ride with Zoë around the hairpin mountain tracks of Crete. Ahzab would drive by gaining as much speed as possible, free-cruise as long as possible, honk, pass on the right and on the left, make two lanes into three, plow through crowds of pedestrians, donkeys, camels, who miraculously avoided collision, hitting the brakes only to slow down enough to twist the ignition key, pop the clutch, and jump-start the engine.

As I climbed the hotel steps, Ahzab was throwing his car muffler into the boot and waving goodbye.

From the hotel room I peered out the window through slits for eyes. Past the newly installed ductwork I saw harmonies of dome, minaret and octagon. A sprawling caravanserai smelling of camel dung and musk. It might be a morning in

Ismailia. It is the opening of the Suez. 1869. The Brits are wearing sun helmets, solar topees as recommended by Thomas Cook, with green shaded visors and neck protectors, blue veils rolled like turbans around their helmets.

The Grand Mufti intones sonorous *fetvas*. The principal *ulemas* of Cairo call loudly upon Allah. The Catholic bishop sings a *Te Deum*. A macedoine of races, yellow, black, copper. 'A Donnybrook *à l'Arabe*,' said the correspondent for the Times in spectacles made of blue glass, blinkers to stop ophthalmia. There's Ibsen from Norway. There's Flaubert's mistress, Louise Colet. There is Gautier eating *Poisson à la Réunion des Deux Mers*.

The two seas: the Med versus the Red Sea. Indian versus the Atlantic. Two seas, two landscapes, two faiths. Britain versus France in the fight for the Oriental trade. A lifeline of untold riches. And there is Yiorgos, a fishing cap in his hard, blunt hands. After ten years of dredging operations, there he is in his caique, amid the royal yachts, Russian corvettes, frigates from Spain, Denmark, Sweden, and the British Iron Clad squadron, now bound via Kastellorizo, for Panama.

27

The fact that Yiorgos and I are promenading through the heart of Bondi is the beginning of a mystifying chapter. For it coexists with a walk through the souks and fortifications of dun-coloured Port Said. Like a dream that wakefulness cannot explain, in which two houses exist, the one as a parasitical structure, and the other as its host, with odd entrances and doubtful passageways between them. Or like the projection of two films onto the one screen, with strange overlaps: now Port Said is buried under roads and buildings of Bondi; now Bondi is drained of colour and trembles under the biscuit light of Port Said. In this psychic force-field Yiorgos and I are returning, approaching something that has always been there.

Unable to put an end to itself, insomnia persists. Under a spell which summons them, men in thin overcoats hang about dark corners. A woman, a wall-whore, going by with hardly a stitch on, sets them in motion like robots. The wall at Bondi with its graffito message: *Stiffie Wunda Numbawun Blackfella Music*, while the pavilion, which trembles as if on tent-pegs, plays 'La ultima noche', a bolero. Ramon Mendizabal et son orchestre.

By now the expensive tans have taken up their posts at the coffee tables on the sidewalk. Every summer new erogenous zones are discovered: side cleavage through cotton T-shirts, crotch décolletage, making torsos one-third mons veneris.

His two eyes set close above the slightly hooked nose, Yiorgos looks at the unclad women on the beach. Women oiling themselves in thong bikini bottoms the colour of Fruit Tingles. I feel his sensuality is bitter and sharp—as in a barnyard animal.

His complexion, which I inherited—monticules of olive and sallow peach—thumbprint of beauty of another race, appears alien here, faintly repellent.

People step aside along the promenade recognising the presence of other destinies that threaten their own, or render them vain by suggesting another take on life. What are they, these people—now that the bias is Bondi—they're psychotherapists from Paddington? Optimum Health and Business Opportunity entrepreneurs from Dover Heights? Beautiful women throw back their heads in a kind of video-ready behaviour that's been cooked in the spiritual microwave of a 'Baywatch' script.

Unembarrassed, Yiorgos fixes them with his eye. Self-enamoured, he turns sideways the better to enhance the oily suffusion of smiling cream underlining the whites of those eyes. Like those young men from the nomadic Wodaabe tribe in the Sahelian steppe of Niger, Yiorgos tries on the coquettish foreshortening of the glance, slightly cross-eyed.

Yiorgos, the body I'm moving in, is not modest about his member. An erection is taken for granted as one of his public rights. From infancy he has the approval of the rest of the family—uncles, aunts, cousins. Virility is the norm and it leaves him stuck in a permanent adolescence—the golden age, when he became a man. For all the trompe l'oeil he's got a cheap but ancient fix on the power of the prick, the johnson, *to prama* ('the thing', in Greek euphemism), clutching it like a teddy. Yiorgos equates freedom and power with the ground he can cover with his erections. Is it mastery or is it obedience in pleasure?

His high-pitched voice has all the citrics of his mother's voice, and belies a sexuality that will attack like a snake, first coiling, then straight, then coiling again on its desert road.

The darkly foreign mentality of Yiorgos Alexandroglou is the glittering eye of a small wild reptile. What it must be like to burrow in the ground. What it must be like to navigate by smell and feel heart-scalding fear scarcely distinguishable from joy. I'm a little overcome myself, how he enjoys his enjoyment, in a sort of eddy of exclamations.

I decide on breakfast at the Lamrock Cafe on Campbell Parade. And realise I'm at *his* mercy. His effect is tidal. We sit next to each other at the counter. He orders a big meal in what sounds like phantom Esperanto. I, a cup of coffee. Coffee? *Masbut*? (Sweetened?) Nubians in coloured waistcoats, baggy trousers and red fez dispense thick coffees from *ibrikis*.

We pretend we don't know each other. When he leaves he takes my check and leaves the one with the large breakfast on the counter. After he has paid the cashier and left the restaurant, I pick up the big bill—flabbergasted. Somebody took my tab! I pay for the coffee. Further down Campbell Parade—although now we are clearly in the counter-realm of Sharia Gomhurriya—in another cafe we reverse roles.

This time it's the Osiris Bar in Port Said, in fact. Kyriakos, its owner doesn't recognise his father and son. Kyriakos is caught between his own father and his own son, like a thumb on both fast forward and rewind. He is a hub of numbness, a vacancy around which other existences revolve. The bottomless source of the future is fed back to the inexhaustible past: his lifeline jams, immobilised in the white noise of spectral recurrence. There is only the illusion that he exists: his face still wears the memorial make-up of the funeral home in Cottesloe. But the illusion is important. It is all anybody has to develop in. Meanwhile...

Meanwhile it's a loop. He's jammed in the routine service of hospitality, like rolling tape thwacking repeatedly against its spool. This is his purgatorial cornice, his samba of death. It keeps his limbs, and those of his waitresses, involved in a monotonous rhythm from morning till night. His hands are frantic, as if lathering them with soap. This spectral life now is like a merry-go-round that has made him dizzy, but with the workaday dizziness of the normal real. See it on fast-forward. Kyriakos, the garrulous maitre d rolls between his tables ten million times in figures as intense as a *haka*. In between children carry large trays of nuts, or try and sell birds in spliced-palm cages to ANZACs. The complexity of its rhythmic scheme is so subtle—intricately moving bobbins banging up against objects wildly at regular intervals. A skinny girl in a tank-top with tats and a tulle party dress pours 20 cent pieces into the juke-box.

I hear the strains of a tango, 'Lamento Gitano', by Joe Loss and his band. Couples slip into side-streets. Cargo ships and rusted tankers pass between buildings of fading elegance.

Yiorgos chuckles, the luminous jelly of his eyes seems to magnify them, making him look fierce. But his voice is surprisingly shrill, high in tone and weak, like a winter sapling. The voice is coming from the head; it doesn't pass through the male glands. For how could he ... he's bodiless, he's dead. His authority remains intact however, even if there's only an after-effect of tan canvas shoes and trousers rippling in ribbed planes as we walk and talk, now along the promenade at Bondi Beach, now along the beach front bungalows of El Gamil beach, Port Said.

The heat evokes for Yiorgos, my grandfather, my self, the old house in Kastellorizo, crumbling in the sun, of fermented grape, and hemp, and the damp hens on the roost, and the neighbours dressed in Turkish inspired *foustes*. Their shrewdness, their dreamlike gestures at the end of the Anatolian horizon.

We'll go there. Together.

28

At the hotel in Athens there was a fax. From Toto.

Hey Dad! Comment allez vous aujourd'hui tres bien mercie et vous? Est-ce que vous et hereuses maintenant que vous est strolling down les boulevardes exotiques? I'm writing the way I speak, aren't I the perfect primitive (primitif). Mum is helping Zoë with the ~~Ban~~ Big Show coming up next week. I'm on the invitation list too. Groovey. Please keep writing the cure, s'il vous plait. Don't write s'il ne ~~plaisez~~ vous plaisez pas ~~pas~~ du tout! Kisses Votre fille cordial,

Toto

I picked up the phone and rang Kostas, Dad's brother. I spoke in Greek. 'Spick in Ingliss, spick Ingliss', he kept saying, but I couldn't help it. It was Yiorgos, picking out rich grammatical structures, showing a skill beyond my grasp of kitchen Greek.

I arranged to meet Kostas the day after next. The general strike in Athens didn't help things. Neither the Green buses nor the Athens metro were working. There was a nationwide stop-work meeting at Omonia Square, where my hotel was. With the banners and the loudspeakers it gave Athens a carnivalesque air. To unwind I walked among the strikers. A fight broke out between two Albanians, gaunt as skeletons. Cops from Piraeus bundled one in the van and took the other to a hospital.

Athens was now a city of rootless beings. Around the edges of Omonia, the refugee faces, ambiguous, disturbing. Many with terror on their faces, like those who have survived earthquakes. Like the eyes of the French boy on the bus in Tangiers, burnt in a drug deal, too freaked to talk, on his way

143

to Ceuta. Pasolini's boys. The country boys who hit the big cities all over the world, from Calabria to Rome, Hyderabad to Bombay, Walgett to Sydney. Cities where they don't know anybody, arrange digs on the off chance, eat when they can. And walk walk walk. I began to get a dull ache in my cheekbones.

I cut out, down some side streets. Cats in the alleyways. Girls arm in arm. Servicemen in uniform. In restaurants, solitary men at lunch time. I check out a 'B-glass' category menu offering 'stuffed tomatoes peper', 'baby lamp', 'boiler fish soup' and 'boiler entrails soup'. I settle for a watermelon slice and started the climb up the Acropolis.

As I head for the Propylaea I think about the questions I want to ask Kostas. About life before Australia, before Egypt.

Kastellorizo had become a character in a tale told by my father who'd heard it from his parents. He never knew the island himself. He left a land not his (Egypt) for another (Australia), not his either. He took refuge on this island, as I take refuge in—what?—a world of ink?

Did all that I heard about the place exist only in my father's mind? I had to find out. Because for me it is as if they had all died in an earthquake, and having met the last Alexandroglou once, the family have left me the entire estate. I needed to talk to another Alexander, one that now lived in Greece.

The strands of autobiography are endless. Endlessly intricate. I could wander around this labyrinth of puns and memories for the remainder of my life. Until destroyed by old age, or thirst. And before I got the total picture, the whole tapestry. I knew that before I began. But it's as if it's the back of the tapestry—all those knotted and rooted threads—not the front, that I'm getting.

Meanwhile the photographers were busy taking snaps of the tourists with their rucksacks and their T-shirts that said *Chanel or Benetton* or some such 'A-glass' signifier, assembly-line manufactured. Other T-shirts said, *Don't Drink the Water / The fish shit in it.* They wanted their pictures taken, here where the houses of the gods were ennobled, where the foundations of Western civilization were laid. Well. What did Mahatma Ghandi think of Western civilization? It would be a good idea, he said. And he was thinking of the British perhaps, whose imperial locutions came from talking with the Elgin marbles in their mouths.

I was surprised when a photographer who was taking pictures of me didn't ask me to buy on the spot. I figured the gimmick was that I would feel sorry about all the film they were wasting, except that they hadn't put any film in the camera. I didn't weaken—until on my way down I was approached by the photographer holding several pictures of me. I was astonished that they had been developed so fast, that he had waited there and matched his bundle of photos up to the faces of the appropriate passersby. Suitably impressed at the initiative I bought a few.

Later I watched myself disappear as the photos turned black. The photographers had just enough time to develop their films, but not enough to put them in a fixing solution. God knows I needed to be put in a fixing solution.

As evening fell I made my way down to the southern base of the Acropolis. The illumination of cities is civilization in itself—the twinkling close-packed grids of the Plaka; then the river of lights from Stadiou down to Omonia, glowing head lamps and flaring tail lights of cars breaking through negative space; the powerful lariats of neon for *SONY, Thomas Cook, 7UP*, of Syntagma; and beyond to the off-lying US Navy warships of Piraeus, looped from bow to stern.

At the base I had reached the 2000-year-old Herod Atticus theatre. Euripides' *The Bacchae* was already being performed. While assorted gatekeepers and managers argued with a latecomer, I sneaked through a backstage door to the pounding of the drums and the shrieking of the chorus. Within my view half the stage and half the audience sitting around the high amphitheatre, and the Acropolis rising up against the shuddering bloodbath of a sunset. A woman is destroyed by her nephew revenging aspersions she cast on his mother's honour. A guileful Greek god establishes his divinity by destroying his human descent on his mother's side. Whole cities ash.

Were there lessons here? I was thinking to myself, when suddenly I came face to face with Dionysius himself, trying to get his Bic lighter to work in the wings. When Pentheus was carried off-stage on his shield, Dionysius complimented him on his performance.

29

The words come slowly, one by one, with long pauses between each phrase, delivered by a plump, pensive man in pin-striped trousers held up by navy blue braces. Around his neck is a white napkin. Businessman back home for a quick lunch. My father's brother.

'At three ... you used to translate ... for your Yiayia. The Australian neighbour ... Mrs Foster ... she would come in and say "Marie, come and have a cuppa", and you ... you would tell in Greek, *"Thelli na pie tsai mazisou, Yiayia"*. You used to interpret for your Grandma.'

Uncle Kostas shifted uneasily in his chair, gazing out for nearly a minute. The brothers never got on well. 'As easy to forget as umbrellas', wasn't that the fraternal epiphany? Where Dad was risk-taker, Kostas displayed rectitude. Where Kyriakos changed cities like suits, Kostas stayed put, observing all the strictures of the island mentality. Migration was motivated by the desire to stretch the village walls, to extend the island beyond the strictures of the clan. Perhaps Kostas felt you could never leave, never make the island disappear; those that left the village merely shifted and relocated its borders.

Kostas himself was now—credit where credit is due—a senior accountant of the National Bank of Greece. And he played the role to the hilt. Dad apparently supposed him covetous of Mum's affections.

Kostas leaned back from the dinner table and stared at the ceiling. Then told an old anecdote about me cross-wiring Greek and English.

'Language can be tricky ... you see ... once when the rooster we had in the backyard pecked you on the cheek ... it left a mark ... a scar ... you see ... and on the bus a lady asked you who did that? You said the pet did it. You meant, *pettinos*—the Greek word for rooster. But it made sense to the lady.'

'Language can be deadly too. Once at school I transliterated beauty spot to olives—Greeks say *elliès*—I had olives all over my face. That went down well at Botany Public School in the fifties.'

'Exactly', says Kostas, opening his eyes and beaming with delight. 'Come and I'll tell you about our ancestral island.'

We sat down in the lounge. With a coffee and a glass of water with *mastika* in it. It was two p.m. when Kostas began and two a.m. when he finished.

So small and distant is Kastellorizo from the centres of Athenian administration it doesn't even appear on the maps of Greece, and was not even counted when the Dodecanese (literally 'twelve islands') were named. Kastellorizo was thirteenth.

'Lucky for some', said Kostas, laughing down his snout.

Kostas said that when Greco-Turkish relations deteriorate, patrol boats scour the Turkish territorial waters, and Greek gunboats blockade the Kassies' unofficial barter trade with the mainland. In the fifties people starved, smugglers were shot or imprisoned and beaten, food—beans, chicken, goats—was confiscated. But the people were hardy seafarers, resourceful. Complicated codes of light signals were initiated, regarding time, place and safety. When goods

148

included cattle and livestock too bulky to travel on a small low-slung launch called the caique, they were tied together with cork girdles (as in the Swiss Family Robinson) to keep them afloat, and towed back to the island over the two kilometres of intervening sea.

These were like the stories I'd heard from the Kastello-rizians in the Hellenic clubs as a child. But as with a relationship carried on by mail, would reality seem like an intrusion, now that the time for an encounter was due?

I flew to Rhodes the next day and went the next 72 miles northwest by boat to the island of Kastellorizo, a barren rock where practically nothing will grow; and yet a mere stone's throw from the prosperous Turkish coastline.

30 We were now beyond Rhodes, on the ship *Panormitis*, beyond reach of the Club Med and Ambré Solaire crowd, with the huge white-capped sea racing away from Anatolia to dash itself to pieces on the headlands, buried in smoke. Yiorgos was with me, a hacksaw between his teeth. The caique sails on through his head. A school of dolphin shivers through his middle. He is on board the *Florou* chugging at full-speed, talking with Dhiamandis aka Paganini aka Sersemis aka Franc, but it is as though all were taking place from a heron's point of view, perched high in the riggings. They are heading for Antiphylon in Turkey. Yiorgos can see the paraffin lamps in the distance and the rowboat at the water's edge and hear the hoarse voices and the crunch of feet on the shingle.

'What's that?' someone asks.

'It's not there really.'

'Where?'

I was well out before I discovered that the sea was dangerous. A strong current was heading off, and I was in it being carried along the western part of the Anatolian coast. The way I was going I'd end up in a Turkish jail. I turned and began to swim back as I could see Yiorgos ahead of me. Head down, he was flailing along with a powerful kick. I didn't call to him, preserving my strength. Then Yiorgos turned, a figure passing through layers of water, faceless for moments. Then the movements of his body across the seafloor were strobed with light, as from some hidden underwater chamber, doorway after doorway casting itself across the lengths of his legs.

150

I woke up drenched with perspiration. A ceramic figure glazed with water running down my chest. I leave the bed and go to the window, secure the blind, and look out, not on Bondi, but Greece: a moonlit heavy-shadowed wall on Kastellorizo island.

31

By the end of the first week on Kastellorizo I had met everyone—population about one hundred and fifty. And I had established a regimen. On those glycerine clear mornings I'd leave my Hotel Paradiso—painted in blue, yellow and brown as if by Van Gogh on lots of retsina—and head for the poorer outdoor bar at the northern end near the civic hall, where the men gathered later in the day. I'd take a bar stool overlooking the only tourist hotel, and write. The little bar with the stools, and cafe tables with their soggy cigarette packets and discarded cocktail umbrellas from the night before, had the louche feel of a hungover party girl.

Along the quay of the port I walked—what the locals call the *cordoni*, hosed down like a ship's deck. Some of the houses were massed darks from the savage mineral presence of the volcanic mountain that dominates the island, others a buttery yellow in early mellow shafts of sun. All had been built before the 1920s, most unchanged since the fourteenth century. The little cubist houses threw themselves head over heels into the blue-green mirror. The reflection of this necklace-like *cordoni* making a broken mother-of-pearl in the calm waters of the bay. Smell of pitch, tar, resin, hemp, sackcloth.

There's no traffic, except the soothing putt-putt of sea vessels. There's no noise but for the cicadas building like little pressure cookers and the tinkling of bells.

Like mine, the island's name isn't its own either—officially it is Megiste. Its other name, Kastellorizo, is a corruption of the Italian *Castel Rosso* or the French *Chateau-Roux*—'red castle'—

152

given it by the medieval knights of Rhodes and inspired by its red rocks. Its towering red cliffs, rising sheer from the sea, do indeed resemble a medieval castle when seen from the distance.

Once, in the heyday of the sailing boats, the place was prosperous from the flow of trade to the Levant, or Odessa—sponges, charcoal, fruit, wine, oil, even pilgrims. Its population soared to 20,000. Then came the steamers, the war, poverty, and everyone fled. 'Elsewhere is inscribed everywhere', I wrote in my notebook, 'in the emptiness of the built environment, in the structural modifications of the population, in the social and municipal structures, in family relations and the concept of happiness in the individual'.

As I write the sun blazes out of the bleached white sky and presses on my rounded shoulders like an iron. Figs ripen and rot, the flies buzz. Slate silence, the rattle of broken crockery among thistle, the ki-ki-rikou of the hens. I write for stretches like this and at the end of it I wonder whether it is me who is writing. A giant fly lands on my page wiping its hands. Two separate universes. I look up and the blue and white flag flaps over the ruined castle, the boat-masts ring, the air encloses me like marble.

> Dear Toto, sweet petal,
> Here I am at last sitting in a kind of plaza. The easternmost of the Dodecanese Islands in the Aegean. A meteorite no bigger than an aircraft carrier. Though stunning with a nearly hallucinatory beauty, the place seems caught between the present and the past, between living space and dead space. Bombed to smithereens by the Germans and pillaged by the Allies in

WW2, you can tell the island had starved to within an inch of its life through the 1950s and 1960s.

I had seen the place as it used to be in the clubs, framed in sepia panoramas in Perth, in Melbourne, in Sydney. Now it looks more like an asteroid, the little sections of Messi Ghialou, Ghialos, Poundo, Palamena and Mercurios showed only the skeleton's grisly grin. As if for icons of dead saints in the Orthodox Church, the old dreamers would light candles to the place.

Because of its phantom existence after the war, Kastellorizo became a character in tales told by my father's generation as heard from their parents. For years I thought it really only ever existed in his imagination.

I have begun some research of my own for the Multicultural Broadcasting Company. I have consulted files with the assistance of the master notary in the National Library of Greece in Athens. In Rhodes I met Illias Collias who provided archeological assistance.

I did some photocopying. Old books revealed antique ramparts, images of walls, wells and mills; Venetian etchings from 1659, examples of coins and jewelry. But the evidence is thin. We know the island was repeatedly sacked by Saracen and Algerian pirates. The Knights of St John set up post here. Suleiman the Magnificent established a Turkish garrison. After World War 1 the island fell to the Italians who controlled it until 1943. Any archival work was hampered by the 1922 fires in Antalya, which was the centre of all the ecclesiastical records, the earthquake of 1926 and the Luftwaffe strafings of 1943.

There is no way to tell my employers in Sydney that this project that I had been trying to shape into a viable reality could be so booby-trapped by a journey that promised to resist recycling into a script.

Kastellorizo now was like some beautiful brain-dead patient, the rest of whose body was doing OK thank you. A forlorn historical accident, a parade route for entropy, a metaphysical junkyard. Nobody on the island remembers beyond forty-eight years. But I've noted some things they do remember. They remember that when the Kastellorizians had to leave the island in 1942 Saint Constantine himself closed the doors of the Church and disappeared. They remember Saint Helen, after her trip to Jerusalem, stopped off and a tongue of fire burned at that spot, leaving a Byzantine coin with the face of Saint Mercurio on it. They remember Dhespina Polycarpou who saw the skies open an instant before her grandmother died. And they remember that young girl, Crystala, who kept seeing a woman in black pointing south: the following week Cyprus was invaded by Turkey.

In Greek, or in a medieval Greek dialect, mixed with Turkish, the locals talk about the Italian occupation, and how the Italians attempted but failed to create civic plazas. They show me a plane tree up to its waist in lime that Italians tried to cut down, but saw an image of the Virgin holding the baby Jesus in the trunk and foliage.

You know, Totts, this is the island where they made that film *Mediterraneo*. They showed it the other night. Funny to be watching it on the island itself.

Papoutsis, the owner of my pension, mentioned, with a downward look, the shifting of the cemetery from one part of the island to the other. Imagine shifting all those bodies? From Aighios Yorgos of Loukas up in the Chorafia to Mandraki. The spirits would be angry, wouldn't they?

So far that's about all I've got. Enjoy the art show. Love to Mum.

In the notebook I write: 'The sea is blue with a grapebloom on it, green, bluegreen silk, indigo mud'. Writing at the edge of the bay with the sea beneath me perpetually moving, my blue pen writing along blue lines. The water's so clear it looks as if the boats are hovering in the air (or the mind) before the eyes. I leave my books and papers on a table and go for a swim across the bay at Kastellorizo. As I dive I see the postcards to my daughter, my wife and the doctor blown out of the back of my notebook and into the water.

Floating arms out resting on the surface of the sea. The mountain silhouetted by the necklace of lights of the quay. I'm free of attachments, in a flux, a million flickering points of light. My eyes are closed and experience whiteness. I begin to hear sounds, a clicking at first as of *tavli* counters, maybe a motorboat far off. And inside that, voices, cries, and horns that roll up and funnel in like some secret earphone connecting me with the creaking movements of past time—separated times, each time belonging to yet another body. I open my eyes and in the shadows, I see Yiorgos, moustachioed and in his youth. Then again maybe it's just the effect of two black sea urchins on the limestone white rocks at the bottom.

32

I received a long letter from Alys. She asks me why all the women are mute in my story. She says it's like Philomela and Procne in the Greek myth. To tell their violent story they must weave it into a tapestry. The raped sister, with her tongue cut off by the villainous brother-in-law, tells her story in the only voice left: the silent voice of the shuttle.

She says I never explain my mother. It's always this father, who in fact spent very little time with me.

My mother was a convent girl. She knew nothing when she married my father, then forty. Even under the best circumstances (and my mother's arranged marriage wasn't) relationships were an opposition of wills; one or the other of a couple was always being gently or brutally, lovingly or violently pushed out of shape. Usually the woman—because it was she who came to married life most untried, the least experienced, the most unsuspecting.

Women, more often than men, awakened from the long dream of adolescence to find themselves bound in perpetuity into some deal without any understanding of how they had gotten there. OK, men suffer too from the condition, but men know what to make of this baptism of fire. Women were left at home.

Alys had a point, without question. The men go away and come back with soaps, smells, raki and ouzo-soaked cheer. But always with the sea in their eyes. Their conversations conjure the dislocated sensorium of travellers: leaping dolphins from the freighter's deck, a pig slaughter in an Italian village, a baby cobra slithering along a beach, fishermen landing a shark. They speak the language of the *mangas*, sailor-jive from the hash-dens of Troumba, Port Said, Aden, the South Pacific: words fall from their lips like trade routes.

I suppose this is what drew me at first. The old men have a directness of mind that we lack. Their message is clear. They jostle for space, casting shade so deep little else can grow. They desire land and thirst for power; they combine humility and pride; seek blessedness but will cut a Turkish throat for it; believe in a sacramental life, but show signs of malice and envy and the rest of the deadly sins.

Things seemed simple. Now we are a bunch of snookered gringos of feminism, with our Armani New Narcissism and our processed cheese commercials. There are no more moral lessons, no conflict, no three acts, no clear-cut resolutions. We go the twelve boring rounds and they declare a détente. We want drama and they deliver sociology.

My great-grandfather Manolis. He was nicknamed 'Dondas' for the time, while steering for the coasts of Africa, he saved a ship by his bravery—climbing the mast and untying ropes, not with a knife or a hacksaw, but with his teeth (*dondia*). He wears a flower behind his ear. Sailors' vocabulary, feet swollen by saltwater, hands like battered horns. His son Yiorgos: Tarzan. Piff-paff, he slaps a thief on the dredging boats of Suez. Then he goes to Panama. But the reality? Deadly green fears, terrible blue agonies. Running short of wind, hair, teeth, options. The sea with its dark and light side. Always weighing anchor, always casting off the hawsers. So little of their longish lives spent together. Just songs of exile, laments and returns. Late night docks, passionate farewell kisses.

It was enough for me to read the names on a poster in Barcelona for my feet to itch: TURQUIA, KURDISTAN, *Sep Oct Nov*, 119,990 *ptas*. EGIPTO-KENIA-TUNEZ-ARGELIA-ZAIRE-MARRUEUCOS-GRECIA-*y mil destinos mas*.

And the women? Left staring into the void, waiting, waiting, knitting their nuptials, vaginas brewing vegetable history, arms in dough, clay, ashes.

I will go and ask old widow Asimina. See if she remembers Florou. Yiayia Florou in her *gouna* trimmed with fur waiting on that thirteenth island of the Dodecanese—*Meis*, or Kastellorizo—transit route since prehistoric times, this pirates' anchorage, this cinder in Turkey's eye. One mile from the Anatolian coast. I find Asimina waiting in a rotting house made of plaster and salt and untidy rags of foam, listening to the ageless wind's edgy harmonies or the sounds of figs bursting.

Asimina is a tough, leathery old bird with teeth that begin at the canines. Her dark eyes sparkle under the grey pergola of her hair. Her left index finger is tattooed. You couldn't tell her age. She channelled and took omens from coffee dregs; she distilled tonics and aromas, love philtres, and powders for positive or negative signs. She removed spells or dealt with overdue periods. She even helped couples conceive, it was said, with a turkey baster.

'*Ta koritsia ine belas. Ochoo, ochoo.*' She laughs, *ta koritsia*—girls are trouble. Alack, alas. They are trouble, 'Ochoo!' She burps out her dialect like behavioural farts, speaks in Fellini shrill and bugs her eyes like Lucille Ball. Girls who prepare the foods of the house for storage. Girls who sift flour, knead and bake the bread weekly. Girls who bring drinking water from the cisterns. The girls washed the family clothes at home and the carpets in the sea. The girls whitewashed the walls of the house, three and four times a year. They made all the clothes and white linen. Some worked the loom. All embroidered, even gold embroidered.

Marriages are arranged. The families make deals sitting cross-legged on thick cushions, around low round tables called *sofias*.

I go with Asimina to the well. We walk along the cramped passages of the village along mostly cobbled streets. *Kalispera mana tu nerou me ti sindrofitsa su*, she says opening the mouth of the well, addressing the hazardous spirit of water. The mother of the water and her friends. Beware the moon-sponsored changes of the *kalatsangarya*—that gang of nutty women sleep-walkers. The women who, despite the efforts of their husbands, dress up and go out at night, who swim, who take the boats out on nights of the full moon. Pretend to go to Cyprus? Go to Cyprus? These I ask about but she simply puts her finger to her mouth and continues drawing the water.

The Yiayiathes in the family maintain the psychic-social life of the island. Practical, but believing in miracles, wonders, portents and apparitions. Divination by mirrors, water, lead. There were the evil eye, the *neraides* who attack the young, the *stringles* and *gelloudes*, female demons who cause diseases in the unbaptised. Theophanies are common.

Asimina draws a semicircle and shows me where Florou lived. The house built where the *ikona* washed up, on Kaos. She shows me a photo of Florou, my grandmother. She is shoved awkwardly into the Kalamaki pine frame like a body in a trunk.

No escape, no renewal. Florou became an overwound toy. Speaking too fast and moving in jerky fits. It was written into the deal and endorsed by the Turkish garrison. The *montsarif* of the Isles of the Imperial Archipelago, Ahmet Atabey, ordered Manolis Alexandroglou not to demand as groomprice or *proika*, more than one horse, no more than a foot of olive or fig.

Can a man find himself in a faded photograph of a hundred years ago, or in his father's look, or his mother's hands? Thinking of my Yiayia and Papou, my pro-Yiaia and pro-Papou, I ask Asimina: 'Does anyone's life, any people's experience, the human race, tend in any direction?'.

I had looked for a book and found Yiorgos Alexandroglou. I looked and looked trying to make sense of things: my past, my father's death, my other Yiayia's death, Philippa's death, Willem's, Linden's, Dominic's, Dooly's—all lost within a space of a few years of each other. I wondered whether the old lady would understand how they left behind a karmic uproar, tearing a rift in the membrane between this world and the next.

Taking my arm Asimina led me through an inner passageway, covered with awned gourds, through a door with a latch and chain to a back room, where private consultations took place.

'*Neler gialdi*, say the Turks, *Neler guesti*. How many people come to this world, how many people have gone … and how many lost in between…'

Her head moved cautiously as if probing the space in advance of her trunk. 'Consider Fate, holding a pen in one hand and beads in the other, links in the chain of destiny. Consider Chance, the faceless one, playfully kicking the ball of the world. The seemingly random events of life form patterns. These patterns change, re-form all the time. But they are always there under the surface. Each pattern connects with all the other kinds.'

'I've heard all this before.'

'Asimina can find the ways to make these bits and pieces come together. But you must cooperate with her. You must let go; otherwise you will be wasting your time, and mine.'

I felt a little spooked suddenly. Outspun on this island post. The room, one half black with lichen, the other half bleached to the bone, looked like it had survived intact from the fourteenth century, and the air felt as though it had been stewed in the infinite case histories of the evil eye. I wasn't sure I wanted Asimina dicing with my jinx. As it was, my life was turning into this unsupportable practical joke. And what made it painful, even sacred, was that it was the only one I had. The air was inanimate as I waited for Asimina. Back in Perth I'd heard of people holding seances when the spirits of the *kadaitcha* men passed by. And, not without some malevolence, the spirits picked some innocent tourist in a loosened tie and strung him up by the heels.

I felt marooned. Probably like so many others seeking counsel. Shuttling between hope and anguish. Pain to know, pain not knowing. Wrong to seek, wrong not to. Wrong to bear, wrong to be barren. Hoping for a quick fix, like a shot of morphine. Accepting these otherworldly messages with mute consent or mute dissent.

There was a pack of cards on an old round table, a couch covered in a red and yellow velvet, a skylight. Asimina sat me down in a chair and told me to relax. I looked at the altar with its chipped plaster saints, melted candles, orange rinds and *mastika* resin, river stones, nail clippings, something like a liver on a silver plate, and a dish of pomegranate, bread, and several bottles of rum.

I wasn't too sure that I wanted to see myself as a character in some large book pecked out by chickens.

And as I had this thought I heard 'cro ... cro', and a real chicken walked through the wall, pecked at some seeds on the altar and walked out again. Was I dreaming this?

Asimina came in smiling with an immaculate candour. The flash of her red tongue put a topspin on my mood. She was dressed differently now. She wore a white tunic and wide white *foustes*. These were part of her *endafia* or funeral clothes and are the most important part of a trousseau. I recalled how Maria, my other Greek grandmother, after my grandfather died in Botany, used to take me to her wardrobe, and show me the clothes she wanted to be buried in, clothes purified in the Holy

Land. This Yiayia went to Jerusalem—a hajj—keying her entire existence on her devotion to the Christian god, the high point of her life, after the death of Aleko.

On the island, explained Asimina, the dead are lain with their heads to the west, looking east. But they sleep with their heads in the east looking west. When the coffin passes by, people throw a plate of water on the threshold of the house to purify it. The windows bang shut and women sprinkle rose-water on the corpse.

Rocking from left to right, said Asimina, she and Florou, like the other *myroloji*, with their unbraided hair swishing, would tap the floorboards with both hands just as in the *anakalima* of ancient Greek tragedies.

Sitting down in the filtered milky blue skylight, Asimina took a swig of rum and spat: *ptousou, ptousou, ptousou.* She inhaled incense from the burning orange peels and resins. She threw back her head expelling the smoke through her nose. It spiralled up the light. She kept doing this in a persistent rhythm. Then she took my watch and closed her hands around it and shut her eyes and rocked. I closed mine. We were rocking between two suns for a moment.

As a fevered child you watched the curtain breathe against the sill. With a mix of pleasure and terror the intangible took shape. Asimina had projected a dream on the incense smoke. Florou appeared standing between the table and the bed. *I need to brush my teeth, scrub them till my gums bleed and I can taste the essence of me, only me.* Florou was talking to herself as a young girl: *Someone has picked me up and put me in*

164

their pocket next to his heart, treasured his found object. My girlfriends are free—dandelions on a windy day. Will I end up on the dressing table with the treasured objects or end up crushed on the stones and washboards? You probed soft wet places and I whispered your name— Manolis—welcoming you in folds of gentle flesh. Ime etho: *I am here. A ripped mouse, safe in the owl's talons, whimpering concordance.*

Then I heard voices. Voices I had not thought about hearing for what seemed a long time, a time measured in depth, not by the clock.

　　—*Cuore caotico delle cose...*

　　—Chaotic heart of things...

　　—*al centro del quaddrato...*

　　—At the centre of the tarots...

　　—*e il mondo.*

　　—and the world.

It was the voices of Asimina and the long-dead Florou. They were at a kind of ouija board, and it was not the table I was holding but a planchette.

Asimina was coercing intelligibility from the words, like a crossword puzzle.

'Can I buy a vowel', I joked.

Asimina handed me a concoction, and said, more or less, 'If this don't cure you, you ain't sick'.

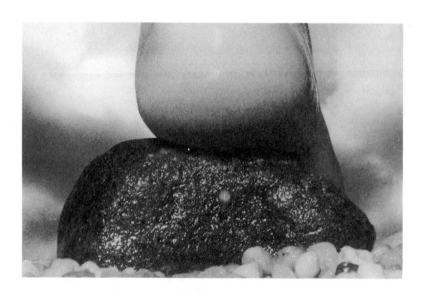

33 The next day, after a deep dreamless sleep, I was heading for my spot at the bar when I saw Inji for the first time. She was doing laps across the bay in her pale green-and-white striped bathers, kicking her fabulous crème caramel legs. A meeting on this small island was unavoidable. Tourists were rare. Inji was a traveller who had been on a sleek Turkish yacht moored in the bay the night before. The boat had left in the morning for the nearest Anatolian port of Kas, slipping through the water, creaming the prow. Inji stayed.

I went for a swim and met her on the stone stairs of the Hotel Megisti, which were half-submerged in the sea. I introduced myself, the sun beating on our backs, half in the water. Without enthusiasm, she introduced herself.

'You're Italian. *Parli italiano?*'

In the soul-dissolving vacancy of noon we talked. Her voice was blurry, sort of shivery, like Mia Farrow's or Melanie Griffiths', rendering dialogue difficult. It was all timbre: shuddery, quivery. As she talked she softly turned from side to side. This slight wheeling of the hips made her breasts dance like the gentlest motion of the sea. With the wavelets, soft as satin on our bodies, lapping. Overlapping. Liquid sounds mingling with the conversation. Body language. The distance *tukku-tukku* of the boats. The water clacking its tongue between the isthmuses of flesh. The underwater currents sweeping, brushing.

Our range of vision is limited to a bare octave of luminous waves, which is a considerable part of the whole range of light heat rays emitted by the sun.

167

Close up her eyes looked narcotised. I could see she was unhappy. She was here to shake off a man, it turned out. Her boyfriend had stayed on the yacht. They had kept arguing.

I told her little about myself. That I was researching a useless book.

'A novel?'

'No', I said. 'Well, yes.'

We dried ourselves and sat out on the concrete in a hailstorm of sunlight. The sky scoured, the sea bleached.

'Do you want some (deep breath) cream?'

My wrist brushed hers. Everyone knows the way the rifts between the sayable and unsayable open up. You try and think of what not to say. Her 'ex-' was a jazz bassist, a smoker of untipped Gauloise (she had stolen his last packet and offered me one), an amateur boxer.

The loose foresails of the caiques cracking like pistol shots made me jump.

She was a weaver who was travelling Turkey to buy kilims. Hands touched velvet, felt the fine hair between the tips of the fingers. She touched and felt everything: slashed fishnet, tangled fishing lines, my white linen towel, old buttons, the ragged edge of curtains. Her eyes closed as the teeth of the comb touched her head, slowly opening as her wrist slackened at the end of each stroke.

Had she profited from her travels? Was it conducive to creative ideas?

'Why?'

'I'm merely interested.'

'You're merely interested.'

Both desperate in different ways, I thought, coming at different angles from the same nothingness to a landscape that was charged somehow, the volcanic mountains of Anatolia in the olivegreen distance with its spears of grass, and flowers covering trees like smoke.

I entered a garden. To cut some fruit. Some mint and some basil. A little maiden startled me. I lost my heart over her.

Would she have dinner tonight at the Ikaros?

In the evening, after the sun had made an ellipse around the island, she was sitting at Cafe Ikaros, in a little orange mini-dress. She was swirling a pale milky liquid round in her almost empty glass. I ordered a *mezethaki* of octopus and olives. Dry now, her hair looked as if it had been cut with a bread knife.

Immediately the little island community was aware of something going on here. That, I—a Kastellorizian from Australia, a Dondas—was embroiled in a shipboard romance. Or so it felt. It was impossible to get any privacy on this small craggy island. How could one cope living here? The smaller the island the bigger the paranoia. Already the fishermen and their wives started whispering over the clumps of the nets. Asimina, with the *mantella* around her waist, and long white hair, made the sign of the cross every time Inji walked past, muttering words to herself. I found out this was because Inji had spent the afternoon reading and sunbaking by the cemetery of Mikros Niftis. Why wouldn't tourists leave the *xtitsia* alone, those ghosts who died violently, who had not found their repose.

Speaking of ghosts, Yiorgos was back, running around sticking bits of saltcod, bits of cucumber, in the mouths of the few travellers. I alone could see sunlight in his bones, the sky through his eyes.

It occurred to me that I would have to get back to Sydney soon. I laid a soft negligent hand on Inji's leg and she turned away. The sun had begun to leave the plaza.

She asked me about this 'yes-no' novel of mine. I told her why I was writing. How it was a cure for this Sleep Problem. And also how I felt about Yiorgos Alexandroglou.

'The person talking isn't me', I explained. 'But he's also not a character like say, Willy Loman. He's really what you might call a persona. When Sinatra sings 'I Love Paris', we don't feel that Sinatra necessarily loves Paris, nor do we feel he's creating a character who loves Paris, but somewhere in between—a persona.'

'*Personne*', she said, 'in French, means someone, and no one'.

Around midnight Yiorgos got up and danced. A cat shivered off, because Yiorgos cast no shadow. The tragic sweeping hanky, hand slapping the heel of the shoe, arms out, the feminine pelvic roll. Then Manolis plunging out of the shadow of the trees with a jigging movement, each holding the scarf of the one before, a loping shuffle. The *kleft* music, like the blues, was wild and savage, sharp and hypnotic, summoning up from below the earth, stitch by stitch. Was it transmitting some enigmatic knowledge? Like a fabric being woven. Like those flatweave kilims with the dancing girl pattern, hands on hips.

170

Gradually absorbed into the rhythm—*ella, ella, ella*—drawn into the dance because of a gravitational law ... it was the music, its force and character outside our two egos and their chains of command, it was the music that proposed the coexistence of the future, the present and the past.

We talked, we drank. Facing each other we didn't know what to say. Like at the deathbed of a mutual friend. We both recognised we had arrived at a limit. Yet one had to say something. She could do nothing. I could do nothing. Whatever was to be done had to be done alone. From this impasse, and befuddled by drink, she took out of her wallet some photographs. Slow to speak she was headlong in speech.

'OK. This is my home in Ravenna, Italy. Everybody thinks I'm Italian. Because I dream I'm not. Those who believe in only one reality call me Inji. They say this one's my father. But I know he isn't because he's violent. I'm not. Somewhere in a valley in Morocco, at Ketama, my real father lived. Do you smoke pot? Pot is like a woman, don't you think? It has a vagina when you fold it; wet it and you get something like a mouth. The real truth is never in one dream, said Pasolini, but several dreams.'

She put her head on the table between her hands.

'I must attend to nature', she said.

'So must I.'

Drunker than we knew, we stumbled into the shadows and walked over to Mandraki, hand in hand. Among the wild fig growing in the ruins. Among the names painted in lime on rubble, or piles of stones. Names written to stall the effacement of the name of the family in the memory of the group. We kissed. Her lips were full of honey. Lips of cayenne pepper. I was hooked.

Near the cemetery at Mikros Niftis, she ran away from me down the hill towards the sea. She plunged into the water—in rapture, or anguish?—as though she were throwing herself off a retsina bottle. I realised I was sloshed. We matched each other stroke for stroke. The body pivots along its axis, face down, eyes and ears lift above the waterline, left side then right side, breathing every three strokes. Bubbles burst next to the ear, laughter of the revellers closer into shore, air rushing in and out of the lungs. And then I couldn't see her any longer. She was going too far out, beyond reach, like a paper boat. A rip was pulling us out. Was she trying to drown herself? In a

panic I pushed further on but couldn't see her. I stopped swimming and allowed myself to be carried along, the strength ebbing out of me.

As always the Furies were playing with the full deck, the total information. The dead grandparents waiting to be completed by the knowledge or actions of their descendants. Was this it? Death by water? This is *it*, a space-time reserved for you, with no one else to see. Reality was hard and strict. In the past I had been spared. Fate, like an older friend, let me fudge the game of life and death, let me pick up another card. Now oblivion was playing unshaven five-card stud with me. It was playing ferociously to win. If I gave up I could go down like a stone.

I saved my strength for one last effort. I'd take my chances near the rocks where the waves were breaking. I started to swim and before long was in another current, a faster force pushing me towards the rocks. I saw Inji's face on top of an incoming wave, gasping for air. Like a child being born, or a mother dying. I saw her body buckle into the wave's crest. Then I felt her arm and we were swept in between two spurs of rocks.

On the beach she was crying, head buried in her arms. Silently I embraced her under the cypress and gum trees. The moon a pale pearl. My arms encircled her. Her breath condenses like the wake of her voice. Exhaling, inhaling. So do all things inhale, exhale. *Psyche te menos te:* your breath is your strength. Conspiracy, breathing together. After this trial by ordeal would a fresh new peril be sought? There was no power to say what had to be said. Could sex be a temporary stay against drift? Or another spiritual blackhole? Even thinking about it made me feel I was rifling her soul for erotic story-telling.

Her body was soft. Her greyish faraway eyes. Could sex be made brand new? Longing mixed with fear. Ay, what fortune to have her here about me, inhale her astringent musk. Was there an innocence to be discovered, here in this old tragic homeland? For the Greeks—those that tried to rationalise ethics—courage was listed as the first of the virtues. Courageous acts, done with risks—risks to one's reputation, one's job, one's possessions, one's life. Courage? I was going weak at the knees. Lubb-dup, bloodbeat of longing, longing sounding, my wrist in the air touches hers, in the electric moonlight.

Can we love more than one person at a time? Of course, but we make this wall to keep at bay these desires. Do we go beyond it out of fear? Horror? My hands were on her breasts. I held onto her from the side, my hands still on her breasts. I was surprised by this strange beast contained within myself. 'Now', I heard her cry, 'now'. Or was it 'No'?

The fuck fell short of passion. We talked ourselves back to consciousness. I thought of Alys and Toto back home.

The young woman's ill-sutured lids had a glassy gleam of grief in them like a sheen of well-water over numbed depths. What was meant to be an ecstatic parenthesis became a crushed cockroach, a row of feet that had been squashed but which continued to move in a crumpled Kleenex.

We left Mandraki separately that night for our respective hotels. She kissed me sweetly and attempted a smile goodbye.

The next day I caught the *Panormitis* back to Rhodes. Filing through the disembarkation gates, my mind kept running back to Inji. I looked down at Kastellorizo, squinting an eye against the smoke of her last Gauloises I found in my pocket. From the breezy decking I saw men in uniform gathered around the police station in the plaza near the steel tower. One man looked up, jerking his head around, and the strike of his eyes caught me in the middle of my gloom. It was Belacqua Toth. What the hell...? For a moment he looked as though he might call to me—sound me out—but I didn't give him an opening.

On board the boat the ticket collector said that a young woman's body, an Italian, had been found at Mandraki. Had she meant to drown herself the first time? Why? I'll never know.

I pressed my knuckles into my cheeks. With a terrible velocity of thought my mind whirled in a narrowing spiral round the experience of the night before. I'd seen dead people before. Lying as still as stones, their expressionless eyes staring up at nothing. But Inji, I could still feel her heartbeat in my arms.

There was nothing to say, and nothing to say it with. And there was nothing to do but lean on the gunnels and watch the cloud shadows raking the sudsy waves of the Mediterranean, and listen to the ageless keening of the black-headed gulls in their bed of wind in the wake of the ship.

I was tired of being an absentee and wanted to get home. My head resting on the throbbing railing becomes a turntable, spinning my body backwards into vinyl iridules.

I am revolving back to Cottesloe to see Dad.

He's sleeping, upstairs above the Seacrest restaurant. The summer cricket's on the telly. Cricket is Englishman's Zen. A short pitch, a stroke, a hit, bat pad catch, a shout. Theme music. I enter the room quietly. In singlet and underpants Kyriakos is sleeping with his face against the wall. Snacks of chickpeas and watermelon seeds. A cremated cigarette. A trail of grape-seeds on a plate. You'd make some woman a wonderful ex-husband, I thought, smiling. But—a guilty thought— I should talk. How many women had I espoused and lost, children begot and lost?

Inside Kyriakos' head are more rooms.

In one he's at a registration desk in Africa, purple black like an eggplant, carved stripes circle his forehead under the hairline, drinking a date sherry. In another—a cabin made of zebra-wood and Australian black bean—there's Violetta at eighteen with a breakable air, a tense plaintive voice, green eyeshadow. A plump wife-to-be with lovely skin who plays the piano and speaks five languages.

In another, the shop in Katanning, a blackfella from the reserve says, 'Thatfella, the debil-debil, sit down alonga scrub, we go alonga sky. We bang, goodbye. Pinish, no come back.' 'That's the Baboulas', answers Kyriakos, 'black belly that eats birthdays. Call him, he slinks away. Name him, Baboulas!'

In another, there's a guava tree planted by Aleko to remind him in Botany of Egypt. Now in summer covered with copulating Christmas beetles and their shimmering casings. Violetta on her toes getting the clothes pins off the Hills hoist and hearing the song 'Can't Get Used to Losing You' percolating from the radio through the flyscreen door, and shouting for someone to turn it up. Armando, her youngest brother, always the clown, grabs a bra and holds it up like he's a lady and starts doing the cha-cha with it, his rear end stuck out. And in the kitchen there's George, that's me, Yiorgakis at three, dressed in black velvet and patent-leather shoes, translating for Mrs Foster (our neighbour), who would come in from next door and say, 'Marie, come and have a cuppa.' And George would say, *'Thelli na pie tsai mazisou, Yiayia'.*

In another, the lobby bar of an RSL, featuring red velvet wallpaper and black lacquer chairs, a woman with blue hair removes a fur coat to reveal a black top covered with leopard print bows. It's senior citizen cabaret night. Everyone waits for turns at the mike. Romantic tenors doing halting ballroom steps, hair askew. A big woman—Mrs Foster—in a white dropwaist dress singing 'Summertime' with a growl, milking every meaningful pause. Mother, wearing a black sweater with 'China Club' written across the front in electric blue, does a shoulder-rolling number rendition of 'Besame', clutching the mike.

Kyriakos smiles in his sleep. George smiles in his.

Around midnight after the last *pollo con pisto* has been ordered and devoured, Kyriakos emerges from the Seacrest kitchen in his chef's whites, and sits down on a stool beside several pensive Levantine emigrants. They will urge Kyriakos to sing, and at first the chef will demur. But after a glass or two, Kyriakos is swept away by the mood. He closes his eyes, expands his chest and the old Cairene ballad lingers on the

178

minutiae of heartbreak, describes the most exquisite of sufferings, then ends with the certainty of death. His tenor voice ululates like the call of the muezzins and the whole restaurant falls silent listening to those grown men cry.

Then I remember the Seacrest's gone. The entire Pavilion was bulldozed just a few years back to make way for a snacketeria. A surfer who looks about fourteen asks to borrow my pen. He and his friend on a skateboard turn to the two girls next to him and show them the pen; the girl with long blonde wavy hair nonchalantly pulls a little address book out of the pocket of her overall shorts. Her friend's holding a giant stuffed Bart Simpson doll. That girl's Toto. Toto in her eternal singlet of navy blue stars.

Toto lolled at the end of the buffet table, seeing little more than the lower sections of moving legs and footwear. All around her were raised voices and bursts of nervous laughter. The Biennale party occupied the whole top of a building at the Rocks in Sydney with spectacular views, through massive studio windows, of the Harbour. Toto spread out the chiffon of her baby-doll dress, and sipped from her glass. Her head felt full of cotton wool already, and the room wouldn't stand still. The erratic movement and displacement of bodies and the din were too much.

Her face was stiff from smiling at Alys and Zoë's friends. Alys wore a pink organza space dress and Zoë, a silver raincoat. They kept in touch for a while there, providing a sort of you-are-here circle on a bewildering map and signalling in their dit-dit-dit morse. But everyone was talking at once in a confusion of voices: horrible cacchinating voices, voices haughty and urgent.

At the best of times Toto could not reach out and express herself in the difficult realms of speech. At parties it was impossible to articulate her adolescent misgivings or the disparities of feeling she experienced. She was left always with these draining non sequiturs. And Zoë and Alys were such hypocrites! One minute they were in a corner making fun of the yuppies filing in, going 'Yup', 'Yup', 'Nope'; the next they were rubbing elbows with them and chatting on about the track record of their dealers. At one stage they were re-naming the top arts administrators after the seven dwarves: Artsy,

Fartsy, Cranky, Sleazy, Beasty, Dude and Yuppie; the next they were bowing and scraping to them like they were royalty.

As the crowds increased Toto melted away before large human obstacles, and shifted into any vacant space that opened for her, sidestepping gregarious and clangorous groups, and letting herself be carried along with the currents that led to the food on the long trestle tables. She grabbed a handful of olives and sandwich cubes and pecked at them in the corner. She'd lost sight of Alys and Zoë after their departure from the arts administrators but found them again with the Theorists, standing by the panelled walls honeycombed with cupboards, listening to long lethal perorations that elsewhere Zoë had contemptuously described as Art Criticism as a Second Language.

Toto tried another sip of the champagne. The mere smell of it made her gorge rise. How could people drink this stuff? Sham pain? Quickly followed by real pain. Her ears buzzed with a dial tone.

Toto closed one eye, and listened to the people talking. Words mixed up with images in her mind. The blurred voices seemed to be setting up barriers between each person, rather than enabling conversation. Some talked in huge constructions, with solid grilles and architectural ornaments; some spoke in complex clockworks; some were fierce zigzags. Others were ornate, peacocky feathers, with trailing curlicues. A bit like the Net really, everyone joining in at random when the circuit hooks in, overlapping in atomised riffs, with no fixed locus, no central switchboard making sense of it all.

It seemed a bit like the art in the show too. The artwork seemed all about this mix of styles, a series on non-encounters: Mondrians in rococo contexts, Cubists in bed with Impressionist techniques. And what's more even though the century wasn't over, the Biennale had reached a *fin-de-siècle* mood anyhow. Like a giant X-ray machine was passing through everything, violent, cold-blooded, not changing the structure, but leaving a different picture. A critic said suffering didn't have the same kind of value anymore. That sounded interesting. But what kind of value did it have then?

Zoë's work was nice. With Mum—the face staring out from the screen, homely and familiar—reposing naked in definite unreposefulness. What was with the neckband, high heels and rumpled bedclothes though?

Two beautiful women both with super-even teeth, one with a shaved head, argued about fur coats, and decided that live fur coats would keep everyone happy. A skinny blonde with extra-taut skin talked to a young man in a leather biker's cap and a taxidermal expression, about being body-searched by a police-woman at Darlinghurst earlier in the evening. 'Will you kindly lift your breasts, madam?'

'Oh what I wouldn't give for a couple of bobbypins, Lifesavers, and two cent coins to come dropping out from under my breast'.

At ten Toto was to be met by Shake, who said he'd take her to the Dead Travel Fast concert. He was late. When he arrived

Toto's eyes were full of unshed tears under a sky full of unshed rain. They left the Rocks arguing.

Before long the DJ started to spin the vinyl. Playing at first, some very cool re-makes of fifties music. No one danced at first, bar one connected-at-the hip couple, who surged towards the rostrum to the easy bossa beat, oblivious to everything, except each other's trancey, sexy smiles. Later in the evening the thumping and pounding started, scattering all but the diehards, the true slaves of the beat.

'No matter how hot anyone is in bed', shouted Zoë to anyone who cared to listen, 'it never matches the dance floor'.

The beat moved and controlled the bodies on the floor. Transmitted from the disc to the speaker, from the speaker to the dancer, from the dancer to the dancer. The DJ creating a kind of circuitry, an automatic community of technological communication, where all sexualities meld into one globule of heat-seeking information. Partnerships dissolved and surrendered to the despotism of the rhythm.

By splicing fast soul songs together into a continuous dance mix the DJ built, shattered, and rebuilt a narrative that evoked the unmappable progressions and mysterious triggers of multiple orgasms. This was what Zoë loved—letting the desiring machine of analogue synths and sequencers free everybody from the oppressive categories of gender.

Alys sat out the next few sessions, drinking copious quantities of mineral water. She watched Zoë, white blonde buzz-cut head thrown back ecstatically, prehistoric prawn earrings a-clatter. A visiting French curator, who was appointed director of next year's Documenta, was elbowing his way towards her with a kind of flabby pleasure. Their eyes met. They smiled.

Alys smiled. Good luck to her, she thought. It had taken Zoë a lifetime's planning to achieve this simple state of grace she called artlife. A self-styled existential space that allowed her to do whatever she wanted, with whoever she wanted, whenever she wanted. She had known suffering and she had known joy of nearly Shakespearean dimensions. Lovers, men or women, were distractions from important concerns. The structure of relationships she found oppressive, lovers were just 'tricks'. The State was not allowed to interfere anywhere—not her uterus, not her drugs, not her emotional bonds. Half a dozen women like that could run the world and make it go.

Alys thought of her own muffling behaviour. It would be fun to hate things out loud, take crazy half-baked unprincipled stands on pointless questions, to pee in somebody's fireplace. But she has clung to a middle way, which further results in an inability to be passionately demented in favour of a singular path—hers.

At least she had given life a bit of a shake and rattled the cages a bit. Cages of the past, her background, her various ways of resembling a yuppie. At least she had learned to ride a motorbike. And she had Toto. And, despite everything, she had George. More or less.

It is said that each is born with a knowledge of the ambush of love, and they spend their lives growing into forgetfulness of it till in one fleeting instant the trap is sprung. It's ambiguous, our trap, our ambush: our only hope perhaps lies in recovering some true memory.

When she looked again, Zoë and the French curator had disappeared into a corner.

Alys joined some of the stragglers at dawn. The sky was spitting drizzle between the tall dark precipices of the Business District. There were no waiting taxis. She started to walk up George Street alone in the teeth of the wind.

36 You're afraid to open your eyes. Like film in the camera the action of light will ruin the things you're seeing, collapsing them into retinal scribbles. On one side, there's Alys, your partner in time, moving around the apartment in shapeless zones of grey, decking herself out for work; on the other side of daylight, there's Yiayia, your long-gone grandmother on a shimmering ocean liner, dressed in *endafia*, those funeral weeds of hers, saying, '*PIASSEME, PIASSEME,* catch me, catch me'.

You're in that state between waking and sleeping. From there you can wander towards either of the two: you can go towards Yiayia in the dream, or to Alys and the morning light.

Somewhere overhead you hear a drone. By a kind of coin-magic, the sun appears over the horizon in the east, and shows through the fingers of the charlatan magician. The sun goes in one ear and out the other, the ocean liner shines in a haze of stars in your brain as you try and impose shape on this shapelessness and give a face—your stitched-up face—to the morning.

But you are dead to the world. The drone is a jet. Only a tired hungover body stretches between you and the sound of its Boeing engines. Reflected on its shiny fuselage is a scaled down version of Sydney, which glides its pragmatic buildings over an undulating lowland whose eastern edge faces the Pacific— flaring red cellophane at this hour—chaffing the rocky ledges to Bondi Beach, where glass glints, streets intersect and tyres of the council trucks softly hiss.

While Alys dresses for work—promontory of bare shoulder, jiggle of breast, soap scent—December is into double figures and through fake snow of stencilled shop windows the cafe owners of the Gelateria take down their inverted chairs, the Vietnamese dentist picks his picks and the Ukrainian barber lays out combs and fresh towels.

'I'm going for the test', Alys shouted from the kitchen, scrambling an egg for Toto.

It all sounded so usual and comfortable and native to this flat that you've made your home for five years. As familiar as the handwritten notes on the fridge: MILK CATFOOD BOOZE TUNA ~~CIGS~~

And then she said—you might just as well have been standing on the crater of the moon—'I know I'm pregnant. I must be.' Between sleep and wakefulness, you reached for your ears to see with. You thought: only with children can we connect with anything anymore so she's inventing one.

'It's hard to wake up when you're asleep', you mumble, 'because you dream you are awake'.

She swept back in, caffeine-enlivened, kissed rapidly both cheeks, left! right!

'Will you get Totts ready for school? Could you collect the mail? And see the doctor, *please*. He's been leaving messages.' And from the door, 'You've got to let me in! You're running away from me and shutting me out. I want to be there!'

The yellow curtain—as solid in its folds as a stone column—suddenly sucked in, and then blew out, letting in the daylight.

Life is threadbare fiction, thought George: large holes, thin patches. He rang the Multicultural Broadcasting Company. He was ready to begin production on *Kastellorizo: The Thirteenth Island.* He wondered about Yiorgos; would he be getting further visits from him? Probably not. How often do they have to keep killing each other? Maybe Old Yiorgos would find someone new to haunt. He had no further plans to see the doctor. He quit thinking about Inji. It was strange to be back. It would be better still to see Toto. It felt good. George Alexander surged up the stairs in Alys' kimono. He opened the safe. The parcel was there, between the ouzo-bottle and the first editions.

Time to open the package. After so many things he had done, so many people he had been, and been done by, George in modern dress, period dress, fancy dress, drag; George in swimming pools, on ladders, in fallout shelters, George backwards, speaking gibberish, doing mime, boptalk. Multiple Georges, collage Georges, schizoid Georges, tragical-comical-historical Georges. He needed an editor to call him to account. Maybe this book is a clue.

'Feels like 40,000 words', he said to himself. 'About as much as any reader can stand, or publisher can afford.'

He pulled open the last staple and undid the book in the manila folder. There was the title. Good title, short. Two words. He flicked through it: empty pages.

So all my life is blank ? The message? That there is no message?

'George', Alys called sharply from the front door downstairs. 'Put it away. Think about it later. Toto will miss assembly.'

Blank pages. From the other side of the mortal divide. A life unwritten, a shadow book, an echo book, a catch-me-fast book. Just as our real dreams are the dreams unachieved that are the double of our real existence.

A book that speaks the silence of the real. Perhaps that was a way to read this gesture from a father to a son. Things are as they are; at the end of every reading there is nothing to read. Live life. A most merciful mystery.

I imagined the effort to reach Cairo, Cottesloe, Kastellorizo posted some kind of message, answered something. Was that it? What you've been looking for, but can never find, is *nothing*? Accept the conditions of life.

How can you quest an absence? an essence? an authentic identity? Zoë Ashford was right; it's a fruitless and selfish quest.

But then this may have been the true object of the whole trip: to be back home as though for the first time. Toto, Alys, Zoë—each in themselves a kind of wonder.

Maybe love is what you end up with after all the long divisions and mortal fractions—the denominator growing steadily emptier the further you carry it, until Fate decides to give you a break.

When Toto opened her eyes she found herself fully dressed on her bed. The door opened with her father carrying a tray.

'Dad, you're back.' She smiled wrapping herself up in a blanket as the nipping air infiltrated the room.

'I have a present for you.' And he gave her a package that she quickly unwrapped. It was a blue boat, a scale model of the *Panormitis*.

'It's neat', she said, admiring the perfect rake of its funnels and masts—just that satisfying angle.

It occurred to George that a real boat is a projection of a toy boat made large enough for a navy commander to grasp. The toy boat is a projection of a real boat made small enough for a child's hand and imagination to grasp.

He noticed she had a copy of a book he used to read to her, face down on the floor. It was one of those books she seized on to solve problems. Life sticks to pattern. The acorn doesn't fall far from the tree.

It was Janosch's *The Trip to Panama*. 'Once upon a time there was a little bear and a little tiger who lived in a cosy cottage next to a big tree.'

George sat down on the floor. And Toto—she wore striped socks on striped doona-cover—smiled with young vitality and briskly started to read it in a sweet and promising voice.

'"Aren't we lucky", she went on, "we are not afraid of anything because we have everything." They were happy. Everyday they went fishing and collected mushrooms, until one day a wooden crate, with the word *PANAMA* written on it, floated on the river. "Ooh, I smell bananas. The whole country smells of bananas and is the land of our dreams. In Panama everything is more beautiful. We must leave for Panama tomorrow."'

Toto's eyes were wide and deep and filled with little lights.

All along the way they meet characters and ask for directions. Then they come to a little bridge. A crow tells them there are many ways to Panama. From the hilltop, the little tiger and the little bear see the house and the river where they lived before. 'Isn't it beautiful! This must be Panama.'

It was the house they had lived in always but had never seen it from up there before. 'Come on let's run.' Then they came upon a road sign—from the old crate—that said 'Panama'. They danced joyfully around the run-down house with the chimney. The grass shrubs had grown and the wind and rain had taken their toll.

'"Oh, everything is bigger in Panama, what a wonderful cosy house." So the little bear and the little tiger fixed it up and made the garden as beautiful as before. "Aren't we lucky to have found our way to Panama."'

'Yes, this is the most beautiful place in the world.'

Toto smiled at her father, and he smiled back. Life sticks to pattern.

Rejected epigraphs

Only part of us is sane: only part of us loves pleasure and the longer day of happiness, wants to live to our 90s and die in peace, in a house that we built, that shall shelter those that come after us. The other half of us is nearly mad. It prefers the disagreeable to the agreeable, loves pain and its darker night despair, and wants to die in a catastrophe that will set back life to its beginning and leave nothing of our house save its blackened foundations.
　　—Rebecca West

The ultimate bomb, the bomb no one talks about, would be the one which, not content simply to disperse things in space, would disperse them in time ... when it explodes, some fragments are thrown into the past, others into the future.
　　—Jean Baudrillard

Generations of men, throughout recorded time have always told and retold two stories—that of the lost ship which searches the Mediterranean sea for a dearly beloved island, and that of a god who is crucified on Golgotha.
　　—Jorge Luis Borges

The past, whether feigned or suffered, is all of one texture.
　　—Robert Louis Stevenson